629.14

TAKING ON GRAVITY

TAKING ON GRAVITY

A Guide to Inventing the Impossible from the Man Who Learned to Fly

Richard Browning

BANTAM PRESS

TRANSWORLD PUBLISHERS
Penguin Random House, One Embassy Gardens,
8 Viaduct Gardens, London SW11 7BW
www.penguin.co.uk

Transworld is part of the Penguin Random House group of companies
whose addresses can be found at global.penguinrandomhouse.com

First published in Great Britain in 2020 by Bantam Press
an imprint of Transworld Publishers

A CIP catalogue record for this book
is available from the British Library.

ISBNs 9781787630895 (cased)
9781787630901 (tpb)

Typeset in 12.25/16 pt Arno Pro by Jouve (UK), Milton Keynes
Printed and bound in Great Britain by Clays Ltd, Elcograf S.p.A.

The authorized representative in the EEA is Penguin Random House Ireland,
Morrison Chambers, 32 Nassau Street, Dublin D02 YH68.

Penguin Random House is committed to a sustainable
future for our business, our readers and our planet. This book
is made from Forest Stewardship Council® certified paper.

13 5 7 9 10 8 6 4 2

This book is dedicated to my mother Sue for being there, my wife Debbie for believing in me, and to the memory of Michael, my father.

Everything we have done while building Gravity embodies his creativity, passion and spirit.

CONTENTS

INTRODUCTION

Location: a farmyard in Wiltshire.

Click.

The engines switch into life. I glance up at the data flashing across the inside of my visor. One, two, three, four . . . *five*! Every jet turbine strapped to my body is operational, accelerating towards 10,000 rpm, 20,000 rpm, then 30,000 rpm before levelling out to 'idle'. The familiar smell of jet exhaust fills the air around me. A growling, roaring sound, like an industrial blowtorch, begins to build, louder and louder until eventually what sounds like an angry hurricane swirls around me.

I'm about to fly.

There's a visceral sense of chest-bashing chaos. I'm connected to, and almost enmeshed with, two engines on each arm with another affixed to my back. Their combined power exceeding 1,000 horsepower – more than a Formula One car. With my weight of 75 kilos, I have a greater power-to-weight ratio than all known fighter jets. But I've tamed that power. I reassure myself that everything is under my control.

Arms to my side, the force is directed downwards and builds beneath me. I feel the fearsome roar around my legs, my stomach and my chest. And then . . .

Calm.

The noise and blast growl on, but I'm suddenly cocooned within a bubble in which I hear only a gentle rush of air. The sound feels distant, though I know I'm in the eye of a storm, and soon I lift, the upward motion starting in the balls of my feet, my weight seemingly melting away until eventually my toes drift effortlessly into the air, inch by inch and then foot by foot to a height of several metres, the thrust commanded by a throttle trigger in my right hand. My body moves ever upwards. To arrest this upward momentum I flare my arms out instinctively. To descend, I lift them even more, redirecting the thrust away from the ground, waiting for gravity to gently work its magic.

I'm in control of a flying machine, able to move at will, with the potential to fly in any direction at speeds of 100 mph to altitudes of thousands of feet – if I felt like shortening my life expectancy considerably, that is. I've achieved what most people can only dream about: I can soar above the ground like a bird, outside of a plane, helicopter, hot air balloon or hang glider. It is an incredibly liberating experience.

In fact the sensation is euphoric. There's a feeling of unlimited freedom. I have complete 360-degree mobility; I'm able to launch myself in any direction. The motion is so exhilarating that if I've been flying throughout the day, when I eventually unclip out of the suit and walk around like everybody else, my movements seem limited, as if I've been shackled to some unseen object at the ankles. I might want to head towards my car, or cross the road, and the first instinct is to fly directly there, until I remember that physics and evolution have put restrictive rules in place. Walking feels heavy, cumbersome. I suppose the sensation isn't too dissimilar to when a person has been skiing or cycling all day. To suddenly have to move around on foot feels clunky and slow. But when in the air it's dreamlike, I'm able to drift away like a bird, as if I were in a 'flow state', oblivious to the constraints of gravity. It's pure and utter joy.

Sometimes explaining the psychological rush associated with both designing and using the suit can be strange. People have, of course, questioned me, certainly in the beginning after we launched publicly. They say, 'You've invented a jet suit? But . . . *why*?' Which is a fair enough question: my journey has certainly been unconventional, having departed from a well-paid and stable position in the energy industry in order to pursue an idea that has fascinated and inspired mankind for centuries, from ancient Greece's mythological figures to a who's who of creative minds, including Leonardo da Vinci, the Montgolfier brothers and Elon Musk – the idea that a person can fly among the birds, or to the stars, with or without wings, achieving true freedom. Fulfilling this dream has drawn deeply on my reserves of perseverance, innovation and ambition, but whenever I drift ever upwards in the jet suit, my flight gathering altitude and velocity, the world racing by below, in what is a blissful sensation, the effort seems entirely worth it.

The feeling of flight is like no other.

So who wants to have a go?

Richard Browning
Salisbury, 2019

1

THE TONY-STARK-IN-THE-CAVE MOMENT

Or, How to Get That
New Idea Off the Ground

was an ordinary bloke, working an ordinary job, with an extraordinary idea.

I was deeply intrigued by the fanciful idea of being able to fly like a bird, without the aid of a plane or helicopter. But not only did I want to fly, I also wanted to reshape how man viewed the concept of flying by heavily leaning on the brain and body: the idea that our neuromuscular circuitry, which has been hardwired to walking, or running, might be reprogrammed to operate comfortably while flying with the help of some power.

Prior to inventing a fully functioning jet suit capable of reaching speeds of 100 mph and generating more horsepower than a Bugatti Veyron, I was a Royal Marines Reservist for several years and became fully immersed in the belief that the human body and brain could push beyond what was believed possible. I'd crashed through what I'd perceived to be my personal limits to pass the Commando Course and attain the coveted green beret. In ultra-marathon competitions I went even further, running greater distances than I ever thought I was capable of, while watching a field of athletes pushing themselves in the same way.

Having eventually left the Royal Marines when the first of my two sons was born, I then replaced the military thrashings with another strenuous pastime: an obsession with callisthenics. This is a style of bodyweight exercise perfected by gymnasts and free runners, not to mention a number of highly skilled athletes in other disciplines, the kind you might see performing at Cirque du Soleil. My interest in the sport began as a lunchtime escape to the gym. I wanted to continue to explore the body's limits in terms of strength and control. I used my physique in an aggressive way at the gym, building the core strength and muscular control to execute a range of movements. Along with hand-stand dips and muscle-ups, I was learning how to hold my arms in two gymnastics rings, before suspending my rigid form in a horizontal position, my body held in place with muscular strength alone, a feat gymnasts call the Maltese Cross – not that mine was anywhere near the technical proficiency of a proper gymnast. I later learned how to 'roll up' from a crouched position into a handstand and perform planche planks, a tricky position where a person's vertically straightened arms hold the body parallel to the ground like a suspended press-up.

At times the effort was excruciating, but I usually managed to tap into a well of inspiration. It struck me during those intense sessions, my muscles and tendons trembling with the strain, that the human form was capable of a myriad of unexpected physical feats . . . *and if we can do all this on land, what might happen if we had wings?* The fictional, fabled retellings of previous attempts at handcrafted flight had been tales of disaster, from Icarus, the mythological character who flew too close to the sun in a winged suit made from feathers and wax, to 1981's Condorman, the goofy Disney 'superhero' played by Michael Craw-ford of *Some Mothers Do 'Ave 'Em* fame. Neither storyline delivered a sequel: Icarus because his wings melted, causing him to crash into the sea and drown; Condorman because his escapades paled in compari-son with those of Superman, Batman and their caped peers.

But the spark had been lit.

What if I could extend my interest in callisthenics into something more creative? What if I built the right type of wing structure that could generate enough lift for me to lean on instead of a pair of gymnastic rings? What if I linked up the weak arm and chest muscles with the stronger muscles of the back and legs, giving me sufficient power to be able to deflect a man-made, replicated wing system? The only way to find out was to investigate nature's solution to the problem, and to my wife Debbie's amusement I constructed a mood board, pinning photos of swans landing, eagles soaring in thermals and artistic impressions of pterodactyls to a cork wall in our spare room. Geese, hang gliders and bats were later affixed to the space. I fantasized about constructing a giant birdlike wing and, as ludicrous as it sounds, attempting to glide it into a headwind from the top of a gentle slope. If I could achieve that, then develop the strength and balance to deflect the air flow and glide further, I could be on to something. I was certainly light enough to give it a go, thanks to those ultra-marathons. I was also strong enough due to my time spent hammering myself in the gym. My only stumbling block was that the equipment needed to succeed was unavailable at that point. Or so I thought.

Expanding on my unconventional thinking, I found a local bird of prey sanctuary and went to get a closer look at how the animal kingdom solved the problem. It turned out that this particular establishment in Salisbury often received injured birds that were beyond help, usually after being injured by cars, and spotted by passers-by. When I arrived, I explained that I was interested in the anatomy of a wing and a very kind lady handed over a recently deceased buzzard, despite the fact that mine was a very strange request and I was a random stranger who had walked in off the street. Excitedly, I pored over the mechanics of the bird's wing structure, marvelling at its stunning aerodynamic design.

The study proved fascinating. I pinned one respectfully removed and outstretched wing to a piece of wood and wafted it through the air, noticing how it generated an incredible amount of lift for its size. What was probably over 150 million years of evolution held me in wonderment – I was both inspired and amazed. The wing remained silent as it moved; I noticed the feathers didn't even rustle. It had evolved around a parallelogram folding mechanism, a similar structure to the one that connects a human arm to the wrist and hand. I was obsessed with how beautiful the wing system was and felt dazzled by the possibilities: could that same system be integrated into a human body, one with a capability for strength and balance?

These thoughts propelled me into a world of construction possibilities. To build a replica wing I'd need material that was incredibly light, strong and flexible. My first instinct was to turn to angling, not for a period of rumination, but for its technology. I knew coarse fishing rods were tough, malleable and lightweight given that they were made from carbon fibre. It was possible to prod somebody accurately with one even when standing 5 metres away. Meanwhile, a wing designed with a web-like structure of tubular carbon-fibre poles was theoretically ultra-lightweight and semi-flexible. The only problem was the cost. Coarse fishing rods were pricey. But the one thing I'd learned about the British mentality was that the weirder an idea sounded, the more disarming, and the more inclined complete strangers were to jump on board and help. So having made phone calls to several fishing rod manufacturers, I drove north, where a distributor had invited me to scoop all the old rod sections from their sales samples and repairs workshop.

As with all research and development projects, most bumps in the road prove both unexpected and unavoidable. After a period of tinkering, I learned through a friend that a somewhat secretive company based in Oxford had started work in a similar area. Animal Dynamics specialized in designing 'super-efficient systems inspired by the deep study of evolutionary biomechanics'. Clearly we were both headed in the same direction, and I was excited to meet kindred spirits. When I contacted them for their thoughts on my wild idea, I was told that everything I'd been looking at could be considered 'entirely possible'. That was the good news. The bad followed shortly afterwards: 'In fact we're working on it right now. Oh, and we're also trying to replicate a fish tail which can be used on a ship instead of a traditional propeller.'

At first I was disheartened. Animal Dynamics was a 'spin-out' industry from Oxford University and was sitting on a pile of resources, both in human and financial terms. I was an army of one working from my spare room on evenings and at weekends. But I also found the conversation to be encouraging: it had proved my theory wasn't so crazy after all; I just had to rethink my strategy because their resources were superior to mine. To use the modern parlance, I pivoted.

I knew through my research that I'd found a subject I was deeply

9

passionate about: the idea of augmenting the human body and mind with minimal technology to achieve an entirely new manner of flight was the sandbox in which I wanted to play. But maybe I didn't need to build a massively complex wing system. Maybe I could explore a form of propulsion that might work just as effectively. And that's when I landed on my next angle of attack.

The micro gas turbine.

M y work soon began to emulate the story of Marvel Comics' maverick superhero Tony Stark, who donned his Iron Man suit in a string of Hollywood blockbusters. In the movies, Stark is a well-meaning but somewhat egotistical multi-billionaire playboy, portrayed by the charismatic Robert Downey Jr. As the chairman of Stark Industries, with its opulent skyscraper headquarters, and NASA-style R&D workshop at its heart, he stood as a beacon of innovation while making a nice target for any villains looking to wreak havoc on the world. As a character, his fictional narrative is changed when he suffers at the sharp end of some of the weapons his company has created for the US Army, and realizes they are having an awful impact on the world. Having literally bootstrap-engineered his escape from captivity via the construction of a rudimentary powered iron suit Stark decides to turn his work to good, building in his home lab a refined Iron Man jet suit with science-fiction propulsive devices in the hands and heels. Interestingly, back in 2007 Stark Industries was ranked at number 16 in the *Forbes* list of fictional companies with an estimated sales value of $20.3 billion, sandwiched between Willy Wonka's infamous Wonka Industries ($21 billion) and the Beverly Hillbillies' Clampett Oil ($18.1 billion).

Unfortunately I didn't have the financial resources of Stark. Nor did I have his leisure time or unfortunate captivity phase. I worked in the oil industry as an oil trader and self-proclaimed technology advocate for BP, which was a demanding role. Also, the problem with inventing an entirely new method for human flight was that it played havoc with a person's sleeping routines. I was terrible at relaxing anyway after long days spent working at BP, my brain struggling to switch off at the end of the week. Rather than toss and turn for hours on end, I got into a strange habit of grabbing my head torch and running across the fields surrounding my home town of Salisbury in an attempt to calm the internal brainstorms that tended to rage when most people were snoring peacefully. With a homespun project on the go, my mind was over-stimulated. I was inspired, and whenever I was struck by inspiration during the night I'd get up, buzzing with a new idea about where I might go next. Trying not to wake Debbie, I'd set out for a couple of hours before returning home, finally relaxed and with my thoughts in order. By now, part of the house had become my equivalent of the Tony Stark cave – the terrorist stronghold from the first *Iron Man* movie in which the captured Marvel superhero plans out the schematics of his flying suit – and I would return to sketch and prototype whatever new ideas I'd had when out running.

Over the course of a few months, my move into micro jet turbines had proved both exciting and terrifying. I soon realized that there are three fundamental considerations when it comes to propelling a person into the sky using that type of technology: power, weight and fuel consumption. If an engine requires a person's bodyweight in fuel to get off the ground, the whole concept is flawed from the outset: the working system is too heavy. The turbine also needed to produce a serious amount of power – the type of engine used to fly a typical model aeroplane wasn't going to be sufficient. Also, the equipment needed to be as lightweight as possible if I was to strap it on to a human body and it wasn't itself going to be an onerous burden to get airborne. Having spoken to an airline pilot friend of mine, who I'd learned was also completely obsessed with micro jet turbines, and been assured that the technology could handle all the requirements needed for human flight, I took the plunge and splashed out about four grand on a single engine, which I bought from a great model aircraft store I had come to know in London. This was a lot of money to spend on something that had all the potential to be forever stashed away in the loft in a box marked 'Richard's Pretty Silly Idea', but without taking that risk I knew I was never going to get anywhere – quite literally.

The equipment arrived in an innocent-looking brown cardboard box, and once I'd unpacked it and worked out how the various components fitted together, I realized I needed a means of testing its potential. At the time we were in the process of replacing our washing machine, and as a deliveryman prepared to pack up the old appliance, swapping it for an upgraded model, I asked them to stop.

'You know what?' I thought to myself. 'I see an engine test-bed in that washing machine.'

A test-bed in this case simply needed to be a robust enough structure, ideally set at table height, from which to assess the engine's thrust generation without itself being launched into the sky. The old washer in the garage was heavy enough to steady my new toy so I built a basic wooden rig to accept the engine. With my micro jet turbine connected up and ready to go, I affixed it to the test-bed with its mounting bracket and, after a couple of hours of not reading the manual, managed to power it into life. There was a slow-accelerating whine at first as the turbine starter motor spooled up. This was soon replaced with what sounded like the roar of a *Star Wars* spaceship launching into hyperspace on an iMax movie screen – I was soon rueing the fact that I hadn't bought any ear defenders, as my hearing crumbled with the increasing decibels. By the time the engine had warmed up, it was as if a *T. rex* was crashing around inside my garage. The noise was unbelievable. Its intensity the sort that provokes a deep-rooted primal sense of fear.

'Oh my God, that's terrifying,' I thought . . . followed by: 'Now let's see what this thing can do in terms of throttle.'

I increased the power slowly with the rigged-up servo controller, not wanting to fire an old Whirlpool Spruce into orbit, and watched with a mixture of childlike joy and horror as the contents of my garage started to shuffle their way through the double doors and on to the drive, propelled by the violence of the exhaust. Bins, wellies and bits of wood tumbled into the distance. The washing machine vibrated aggressively. Not put off, I dialled in the max 117,500 rpm to deliver the full 22 kilos of thrust. To my amazement, and horror, the washing machine started to tip. I quickly backed off the power to idle, avoiding a proper garage re-arrangement, but this had been quite a moment. My expectations had been exceeded. This innocent 1.5 kilo biscuit-tin-sized cylinder, when awoken, was capable of opening the gates of hell. Clearly, if I combined several of these engines I'd have enough thrust to propel a person into the air. I tapped the 'off' switch and powered down the micro jet turbine.

Debbie appeared from the kitchen, watching me with an excited look on her face.

'Richard, that's really cool,' she said. 'Now, never turn it on around the house again – the neighbours will wonder what on earth caused that racket.'

She was right. It *was* cool, and it was also an anti-social behavioural order waiting to happen, but at least I was in a position to make some creative forward leaps. Knowing I had the method with which to take a person into the air, I now had to harness its force in such a way that it became controllable and, more importantly, user-friendly. The most logical step appeared to be to build a pair of handheld devices that connected several engines to a pilot's arms, rather than the jetpacks of sci-fi legend, where people controlled the speed and direction of movement by waggling joysticks that adjusted nozzles attached to a pilot's backpack engines. My only problem? I was unsure of exactly how many engines I'd require to become airborne, where to place them, and whether it would be possible to achieve balance and control.

I went to work.

Nobody in my day job was told about my plans; I only mentioned the developments to a handful of close friends, people I knew wouldn't be too surprised by what I was up to. Throughout my life, I've adopted the attitude that actions speak louder than words. I've never wanted to talk about what I *hope* to achieve. Instead, I've preferred to make one or two forward strides into an idea so it becomes tangible. This, as I understood from the outset, is an important step for any innovator, especially one looking to make progress in an uncharted area like this. It is also important to stay motivated and persevere despite the commitment of a day job. Having a physical 'something', some newly constructed equipment, say, or a written piece of software – the first step towards realizing an idea – helps to remind a person that the idea and the path they have undertaken are real. It's a process I've become accustomed to. Whenever I've been struck with a concept, I've always tried to move quickly. I once designed an item of military clothing while at university and immediately gathered together the raw materials required for its manufacture (see chapter 7). Working with haste while producing tangible results, rather than relying on imagined outcomes, created a sense of momentum, encouraging me during those times when it might have been easy to become distracted, or lose focus.

After some homemade construction and tinkering, Mark One of the prototype suit was ready, with a massively over-engineered aluminium arm assembly that held the micro jet turbine in place. By slipping my hand into the ugly and rather heavy structure it was possible to hold a single turbine and control the throttle. In a way it was a bit like holding a very powerful hairdryer, and my long-term plan was to have a sleeve on each arm, so I could bring directional balance to my system. I wanted a set-up where the engine never came loose from my grip, and tested the concept with a single engine on one arm. I knew I needed more power, but also had to balance the distribution of it so the thrust would travel directly up my arm, rather than cocking it over to one side. Having two engines on each arm was the logical solution.

Whenever I was at home, the aluminium monstrosity on my desk reminded me that I wasn't engaged in a menial task, like doing my tax returns, or filing bills . . . *it told me I was building a jet suit*. Enthused, but somewhat scared of annoying the local community with my next round of testing, I took the equipment to a friend's house where there was a large expanse of open grass that backed on to a small row of allotments. This time the turbine wasn't bolted to a washing machine: it was intimately connected, via my crude construction, to me. This felt like a landmark moment, and frankly not one recommended in the owner's manual. Having fired up the engine to idle I gingerly tweaked the servo controller throttle dial. A moment later I felt the acceleration of the turbine and the corresponding surge back up my arm as the power increased. Another tweak and the jet exhaust was shredding grass and picking up turf 20 feet away and I could barely brace myself against the brutal, unrelenting energy. Imagine a fire hose pushing you away from where you point the jet of water. I knew I was on to something. The force on my arm was mind-blowing but the surprise was the level of control – there was no gyroscopic effect fighting me as I moved it from side to side; the sensation was almost soft and spongey. It clearly wasn't enough to take me into the air just yet, but I knew that with several more micro jet turbines attached to my body there was a good chance I would get airborne.

The friend who had kindly let me abuse his field in the name of science gestured to a dilapidated garden bench next to where we were testing, and gave the thumbs up.

I aimed the Mark One engine assembly at the weather-beaten wood and turned the throttle to full blast, bracing myself against the 22 kilos (48lb) of force. Within seconds the rotting structure had been dismantled and spread across the field. I knew that if all else failed I might be making headway in the demolition business.

I had the power.

By March 2016 our spare bedroom had become a makeshift workshop where I tinkered with bits of aluminium and plastic, pinning more and more inspirational photographs and designs to my mood board. I bought more engines. With a strange nocturnal routine in place, it wasn't unusual for Debbie to wake in the morning to find an empty space in the bed beside her, my work having taken me through the early hours and into breakfast. I'd then stagger into the City, where BP was based, bleary-eyed and exhausted but adrenalized by the progress I was making at home. Unbelievably, I didn't injure myself – not once. I had a decent understanding of the engines and the risks of using them, and managed to avoid the ever-present threat of burns, bruises and breaks. I continually tested, retested and refined my ideas, and my modifications were self-made. As far as possible I wanted to build with existing technology and materials that were within my reach rather than ordering any custom-built products, having realized that for a project of this kind there was no need to spend tens of thousands of pounds building equipment from scratch, not in the early stages anyway. I was so keen to get on that I hated waiting for people to deliver new equipment and was aided significantly by a few keen friends who were proficient in the electronic control systems needed. I pressed ahead.

Meanwhile, I'd found some happy helpers when looking for test sites. One weekend I dropped one of my mini jet turbines into the passenger seat of the car and with a Google Maps printout to hand drove to all the local farms that I'd identified as having open areas of concrete. Unconcerned by my somewhat unusual request, I managed to secure the use of one farmer's remote yard to run some more tests. I guess their reception had a lot to do with the Brits' affection for eccentricity. Who could say no to a man showing up unannounced in search of a space where he could test his crazy idea for a jet suit?

At times the work teetered between hilarity and infuriation. As one handheld engine became two, I rarely caught much in the way of air – testing sessions involved me bouncing up and down on the spot like a pogo stick, as I eased up the power of the turbines. But those were the good days. Innovation is mostly about failing and I did an awful lot of that. Many weekend test runs would involve aborted start after aborted start, with a myriad of causes: loose wires, an overly cold fuel supply, cold batteries, unwanted air in the fuel lines. Welcome to trying to do something new and uncharted. At first I experimented with 40 kilos of lift, a turbine on each arm operated by a crude throttle switch I'd positioned inside the metal sleeves. Given that I weighed 75 kilos and the equipment so far weighed another 10, this wasn't enough to fire me into the air, but whenever I jumped off the ground I'd find myself suspended for a split second before drifting slowly back down. Friends came over to witness the power of what was becoming something of a crazy beast, marvelling at the visceral energy and thrust I had created as we fired up the equipment in the farmyard.

However, for all the exhilarating moments when I sensed the technology's potential, new frustrations and challenges arrived. With the engines up and running, how many more would I need? And where should I position them? With several engines running at once, where should I put the fuel tank? And so on. There was a DIY spirit to everything I did. Every night I took on one of these challenges, working to solve a particular problem in the house before taking my rejigged technology to the farm at the weekends. There, I would test out any new changes and inevitably learn hard lessons about what did and didn't work, all the while familiarizing the resident cows with the sound of jet thrust. In order to hold the electronics in place, so that I could control the suit with a series of handheld buttons, I used a succession of Tupperware boxes from the kitchen, the kind available from any supermarket. I crammed the whole control system and starter batteries inside and drilled holes into the container so the power and control lines could feed into the suit, zip-tying the whole thing down. I then gaffer-taped what was the central electronics system to my back and, hey presto!, I was ready to go.

For months there were countless experiments, and I learned from every failure, of which there were plenty. I attached myself to safety harnesses and took flight from a variety of launch pads. I moved from two engines – one on each arm – to four, which really upped my power levels. It was then that I decided to play with the idea of strapping two engines to my legs. After all, if it had worked for Robert Downey Jr's Iron Man character, then it was worth giving it a shot. I soon had the required levels of thrust for flight, but the results were a challenge. All the hot air expelled from my leg turbines at speeds of 1,000 mph only a few centimetres from the ground, which created havoc. On more than one occasion the concrete beneath me was chipped away by the force. The resulting debris was then sucked back into the engines, doing major damage. For a frustrating period I was grounded while the micro jet turbines were sent away for repair.

The crashes were numerous, but from no more than a few feet and always valuable learning opportunities. One afternoon, as I bounced around the farmyard, the engine system shut down unexpectedly, throwing me to the floor. It turned out I'd pinched one of the fuel lines in the crook of my arm as I'd moved. The challenges were never-ending. Once I'd worked out how to create a portable fuel tank that was strapped to my back, I needed to figure out where to put the batteries. Then, with the batteries in place, to make sure they didn't become disconnected at any point, because a break in the system inevitably resulted in engine shutdown and another nasty tumble. Everything was done by trial and error, and every little error became a learning opportunity.

There's a lot of nonsense written about failure and how an innovative mind should embrace the pain. That's rubbish. Nobody *enjoys* failure. Nobody *chases* failure either. Not in real life anyway. But when failure occurs, a person has to be able to survive the frustration and heartache that inevitably follow in order to learn and to grow. In those dark times – when my fuel lines had failed, or if I was being dumped on the ground having placed the micro jet turbines on my arms in a new position – I took solace in the fact that if I wasn't failing I wasn't trying hard enough. I needed to push towards those murky limits where accidents happened and things went wrong, as long as those failures were survivable.

Before long I began to make rapid progress because throughout the early development stages I had lots and lots of little failures that didn't derail me for too long. Every time a part broke or stopped working I was usually in a position to repair it quickly; I was often immediately able to have another go after one of my setbacks. These experiences became a vital part of my learning process, a bit like for a baby bird when it falls out of a nest. Rather than immediately flap its wings and soar off into the sunset, a fledgling will land on the ground with a thud. Then it usually climbs back into the branches to have another go, and then another, until it figures out how best to fly. Likewise, I was learning too, figuring out where to position the engines and how to hold my arms as the horsepower at my fingertips – an amount I only later measured as being greater than an F1 car – coaxed me into the sky.

And then in October 2016, after seven months of part-time but brutal R&D, my breakthrough moment arrived.

I was using a pair of handheld arm assemblies comprising two engines on each arm, with a further turbine strapped to each leg. I'd tinkered with the leg mounts, protecting them with a system that minimized the debris blowing back inside. I knew I had enough thrust for some serious upward movement; my only challenge was control. But after many attempts at mastering the balance, in that farmer's yard that day, a bright blue sky overhead, I pulled on the suit's throttle trigger, feeling the power building in my arms. The engines roared towards full power, the thrust growing as I slowly and gently rose into the air. I sensed my body drifting upwards as I moved forward. I looked down. *I was a few feet off the floor! I had cheated gravity!* And then, for six brief, delirious seconds, I flew forward in a smooth journey of several metres before landing gently on the ground.

I had done it!

The adrenalin surged through me. My heart pounded hard. Those sleepless nights of work and self-doubt had been worth it – I could fly a homemade jet suit put together primarily in a bedroom.

I felt euphoric.

Workshop Notes

MAKE YOUR FAILURES SURVIVABLE

A Formula One driver trying to test the limits of their car needs to spin off the track every now and then. If they don't, it's unlikely they're pushing the limits of what their machine can truly achieve. They aren't trying hard enough. Likewise, if we embark on an ambitious project and cruise through smoothly, without any hitches or frustrating bumps in the road, it's highly likely we're not pushing ourselves to those challenging boundaries.

As we know, the trick with failure is to learn from our mistakes, and the only way of doing so is to have accidents and setbacks, but to make them survivable. To extend the Formula One analogy, if a driver were continually to push their car so hard that they then slammed it into a wall, rendering it inoperable, their chances at having another go might become limited. They might even injure themself, or lose their place on the team.

My failures were numerous, but deliberately small-scale. On one display flight during 2017, at WIRED Live in Tobacco Docks in London, I picked up a burn the size of a golf ball on my arm. I'd been wearing a leather jacket for both style and protection, but to get my arms into the engine mounts I'd had to modify the sleeves. One of them had rested in an unusual position upon an engine casing's cooling duct. The low-pressure zone created around the intakes of the engines bizarrely drew hot air from the engine body up my sleeve. The pain was noticeable but manageable during the event, a bit like a boxer whose broken nose feels like no more than an inconvenience during the fight but becomes bloody painful afterwards. I now have a small scar on my right arm that shows up particularly when I get a tan, thanks to what became a very uncomfortable injury. On another occasion I knocked a battery cable loose while moving around too much. This caused an engine to shut down, sending me to the floor with a bang. Luckily I was barely a foot from the ground at the time.

Both setbacks were painful, but not so bad that I couldn't press ahead with my efforts, tweaking and improving the flight system in an effort to avoid the same incidents happening again.

Throughout the time spent trying out designs of the suit, I tested my limits, but not so far that I wouldn't be able to fly again. I didn't push myself to dangerous altitudes or jump from high buildings, breaking my legs in the process. I didn't spend so much money that I risked my ability to continue. I'd saved for years to build a financial safety net for myself, which gave me the freedom to experiment. By doing those things I was able to get up after the falls and dust myself down. I could just about afford to spend time and money doing that again and again and again.

By making my failures survivable, I was able to learn super quickly.

O nce the six-engine suit began to take shape my youngest son Thomas came up with a name for it: *Daedalus* – a reference to the figure from Greek mythology famous for constructing a pair of wings for himself and his son Icarus, for a flight that was only partially successful. Having been imprisoned in Crete, the inventor built these two sets of wings from feathers and wax. During an escape in their homemade appendages, Icarus became over-excited and flew too close to the sun, his wings melting in the heat. He then plummeted into the sea and drowned. But Daedalus was able to soar to safety. Despite the rather miserable aspect to the story, Daedalus was a renowned innovator and craftsman so we embraced Thomas's idea. The title was another step towards the suit becoming a finished prototype.

But despite this progression there were countless moments of doubt along the way. I remember laying out my kit in a field one day, surveying the engines, aluminium frame and fuel tanks lying before me, and estimating that I had blown nearly twenty grand on a project that might end up as nothing more than a chapter of eccentricity in my life story. I bombarded myself with questions: Just how ridiculous is this? Where am I going with it? Really, what's the point to all of it?

I was also inevitably sacrificing time I could otherwise have been spending with Debbie and our two sons. I was working my arse off in a regular job from Monday to Friday and coming home to tinker away in my garage, which had been converted into a fully functioning workshop, meaning our spare bedroom could go back to its original purpose. At weekends I'd be out in the farmyard relentlessly testing and tweaking the suit. My flights were getting longer and faster, and various friends and family members would come out to film the action with their phones. Every now and then Debbie checked in to see if I was OK. She was supportive, but her tone was naturally hesitant. It said, 'Look, I'm not going to stop you, but . . . what are you doing? What is this?' At times we were both of the same mind, with no real idea about how far my idea was capable of going. It was childlike, for sure. I was falling over a lot and everything looked a little weird. I'm sure a lot of people wondered why I hadn't spent all of that money on a lavish family holiday, or a nice new car. And I saw their point, because my project had absolutely no certainty of success, and what would success look like anyway?

Most people go through life with a series of objectives for the day or week ahead. They get up and have breakfast. They clean their teeth and get into the car for work. They solve problems, take meetings and make phone calls. Hopefully, if they do those tasks successfully enough they'll eventually achieve those objectives before moving on to the next series of goals. But my experimentation was a journey without a specific, nailed-down target. I knew I wanted to fly, but why? *Why bother?* It was clearly a little dangerous and there seemed to be no practical use for my design. It was just a ludicrous challenge.

And then I realized that was the whole point: I *wanted* to work on something that was ludicrous and fun, for the pure joy of the challenge.

Once we've paid the bills and made enough money to feed ourselves and our families we're driven to do other stuff because it's entertaining, exciting and cool – *it's ludicrous and fun*. Bungee jumping – what's the point? *Love Island* – what's the point? Shoot-'em-up video games – what's the point? When it comes to amusing ourselves we're happy to waste our time in the pursuit of release and relaxation, but when a similarly minded project revolves around science, technology or engineering, that same spirit is often mired in scorn and derision. People ask, 'Couldn't you invest your time and money creating something more worthwhile?' when they should be getting excited instead. Mankind hasn't got anywhere by sitting still and wailing, 'Why bother?' Rather, our childlike inquisitiveness has driven us to some of the greatest innovations the world has ever seen.

So who knew where my mucking about might take me?

Workshop Notes

USE EXISTING TECHNOLOGY TO SOLVE A NEW PROBLEM

As I overcame the challenge of flight by using existing jet turbine technology, albeit somewhat modified, I stumbled into new problems. Rather than allow them to set me back for too long, I looked at how they had been solved in other industries and followed the same path.

For example, as the suit progressed and I built on my flight performances and system improvements, I worked very hard at bettering the fuelling set-up. In the early stages we used solid-fuel tanks, which were very different to the airtight bladders we have now. Initially they were plastic fuel cans, the type you would use to fill up your car in an emergency. They were problematic because whenever I jumped around, the fuel sloshed around too. That allowed air to enter the fuel lines, interrupting the very precisely managed flow of fuel to the engines, which then caused the engines to shut down. Hardly ideal.

At first I tried all sorts of baffles to reduce the problem, including a perforated solid sponge that sat inside the tank to stop the liquid from swilling around. But then I was struck with an idea: think what other industries have used sensing equipment to detect air bubbles. And then it hit me. *The medical industry!* The last thing physicians want when they are treating patients with intravenous drips is for air to enter the feed, because it's disastrous when that air enters a person's bloodstream.

I contacted a medical supply company, who told me they often used optical bubble sensors: when an air bubble is trapped in an IV line it triggers a sensor. They were intrigued and happy to send me some samples, and within a week or so a little red LED light affixed to my crash helmet was positioned in front of my right eye. It flashed red when air from one of the fuel tanks was about to hit the engines, giving me a three-second response time to land as quickly as I could. I had taken a new problem and found inspiration in an experienced and efficient industry.

Takeaways

- Make failures survivable. We should always push our ideas to points where they might hit setbacks or disappointments because that's the best way to test the limits of our innovation, and to learn and build on that vital knowledge. However, we shouldn't push things to a point where our experiments cause irreparable damage, or we can't get up and have another go.

- Don't tell the world about an idea immediately. Instead make one or two forward steps so it feels more tangible and credible. It's hard for people to become excited about a project that is all talk and very little action.

- We mustn't become disheartened if somebody has beaten us to the punch on an idea or concept. Instead treat it as a reassuring sign that you're on the right path. I could easily have lost interest once I'd learned that Animal Dynamics were trying to create a new method of flight. Instead I treated it as an indication I was working in the right area. I stayed flexible enough to pivot my idea, moving away from my plan to build carbon-fibre wings into working with micro jet engines.

○ When looking to solve a particular problem, ask how a very different industry has risen to a challenge of a similar nature and take inspiration.

THE ANATOMY OF
A JET SUIT

Or, How to Build a Flying Machine with a
Baby Carrier and a Broken Electric Drill

Even though we now live in a world where nearly everything is disposable and it's not worth taking the time and effort to repair a domestic appliance, I've always happily preserved such objects, knowing they might help me with the research and development on the jet suit. For example, during a recent clear-out in the house I came across an old vacuum cleaner. I couldn't bear to throw it away so I stripped away the plastic, retaining an aluminium tube that connected the head to the rest of the machine because it was a very good-quality alloy. I know it will come in handy further down the line.

I love the idea of keeping hold of a useful 'thing' just in case it has an unknown purpose or provides critical inspiration in the future, and reassuringly it often does. When a very young relative of mine accidentally knocked my Bosch electric hammer drill into a nearby pond one weekend in 2016, rendering it useless, I retrieved it and realized the trigger system still worked. Having pulled the thing apart, I incorporated the trigger module into the handheld engine system as a throttle mechanism; it operated so effectively the trigger remained in place for ages. In fact, at the tail end of 2017 I was still using it. I remember looking down at my equipment as I was launching at an air show and thinking, 'Hmm, am I really still using a hammer drill trigger that was pulled up from the bottom of a pond? I should do something about that . . .'

My ethos throughout the construction of the jet suit has been simple: I've wanted to advance through the research and development process at home, and with speed, rather than spending thousands of pounds outsourcing custom-made parts that might be discarded as a bad idea after the first round of testing. If I knew of cheaper, more accessible resources that did the job 70 per cent as well I'd initially use them instead, later commissioning a customized, upgraded version if our prototype had made it through the testing phase.

A very good example of this would be the structure we experimented with in the early days to support the arm engine assemblies. Rather than build an exoskeleton from scratch at huge cost, we instead ordered a couple of cheap pop-up tents, the kind that unfold when thrown on to the floor (in theory). I'd realized that the fibreglass rods which make up the inner frame of the tent were super-flexible, strong and, most importantly, predictable in how they kept their shape. I was able to bend them over my shoulders, plug them into the engine assemblies and deliver a support structure that was much more effective than a mechanical jointed system – one that would probably have been heavy, likely to jam and would have cost an unacceptable amount of time and money. We have since solved the underlying support problem without the need for this structure, but it's a good example of accessing solutions from the most unlikely but immediately available sources.

Sometimes Debbie must have wondered what on earth I was up to, especially when a consignment of unusually shaped packages arrived at the door. For example, I once went through a phase of buying rucksack-style child carriers because it turned out they were perfect prototype structures to hold the fuel system and later the rear engine. I realized that if someone needed to place a heavy piece of equipment comfortably across their back, then the basic structure for a child carrier would be ideal, especially once the bells, whistles and Wet Wipes holders had been stripped from the exterior. It became a central component of many of the early jet suits.

Sometimes we assume that starting from scratch whenever we begin a new project or venture is the best approach; that our new designs must come with custom-fitted parts or that we need to work with specific tools for specific jobs. We invest in special microphones for recording projects, or fancy cameras, when our smartphones work almost as well. We custom-make fittings and parts when a quick look on eBay might find us something just as effective, and for a fraction of the cost.

Sometimes I'll just go online and type in a series of words that roughly describes the thing I'm looking for. While researching how best to build a deployable wing for the suit, I typed in the words *folding scissor + hinge mechanism + heavy load + heavy duty*. Pages of random pictures pop up, usually of things I'm completely clueless about. I'll then click on the images and read the descriptions until I stumble across something that might be viable because it's part of some other mechanism. In this example, it would be a folding ladder: a hinged structure used to taking heavy loads.

It's helpful to always work out the basic functions of what we need first and then look for a product that would suit closer to home. The process can save us invaluable time and money, and that very philosophy was in place when I started building the jet suit.

Beside my Salisbury home now stands the purpose-built Gravity Industries creative hub. It's about twenty yards from the garage that played host to the noisy test-bed experiment featuring my very first micro jet turbine. Many versions of the suit have been designed here and it also houses a very modest, portable, pub-style bar, which has been made using the engine cowling from a Sea King helicopter. The equipment inside ranges from the old to the futuristic: some of the tools are from my late father's own workspace and are probably fifty or sixty years old; in one corner we have a small 3D printer capable of constructing prototype parts for the jet suit. It's a great place to be creative in.

There are other points of interest, too. The very first arm mount for the suit has pride of place on one wall, as do an early pair of boots and leg engines which were used in the prototype phases. In fact, the entrance to the building most resembles an installation from the Science Museum. There are various working suits displayed in a mini hangar, including one owned by an anonymous buyer who likes to fly it when he's in the area. Like a lot of people, this particular individual had previously approached me, asking how much it might cost to buy a suit. But unlike most potential customers, they hadn't baulked at the $440,000 price. I'd even tried to dissuade them at first because we were so busy with R&D and public events, though I could tell they were going to press me regardless.

Over the course of a phone call it became clear that we shared a similar outlook, as well as the same dogged determination, so I eventually relented. Within a few days the deposit had been transferred into my account.

If it wasn't for the fact that some rather futuristic-looking jet suits are hanging from the wall, the interior of this building most resembles a fancy-looking engineering workshop. We even have a huge Merlin turbine wheel on one wall, a thrust duct from a Harrier jump jet on another, and the front-end stator blades from a Harrier converted into an enormous light fitting hanging in the entrance lobby. It's inspirational in a way: strangely the Harrier is the closest aircraft in terms of flight mode to what we do, in that it lifts and takes off vertically by vectoring thrust. Luckily, the engines we use are a fraction of the size. When I'm not flying the suit, or travelling to flight demonstrations and tech conferences, I spend the most time here with my team. I guess it's become part office, part playground.

It was in this building that over many months we upgraded the suit capable of flying me across a farmer's yard for six seconds into a machine capable of five minutes of flight time, recorded speeds of 90 km/h (I know it can go much faster) and with the potential to reach a height of thousands of feet (though everything has been tested at a sensible altitude so far). At this place, I've developed the suit from an idea that nobody thought would work into a profitable business, with the potential to expand to a scale I never thought imaginable. So much of what I've done was unimaginable at the beginning. My drawings and ambitions were the preserve of films and comic books, and

I've certainly come to appreciate the impact science fiction has had on the world of innovation.

In 2017 I was invited to Comic Con, which as the name suggests is a convention for comic-book fans, a truly massive annual event held in San Diego. Apart from the considerable irony that among the aficionados of Iron Man and a raft of other flying superheroes I was the only person in attendance with a suit that *actually worked*, I came to realize that science fiction and fantasy is very appealing to humanity, especially when the news headlines surrounding us are so bleak. It's escapism, a space where we can dream and imagine things that are never going to become a reality.

And yet, sometimes they do.

We are developing driverless cars, as originally depicted in films such as Arnold Schwarzenegger's *Total Recall* three decades ago; we have developed drone technology that is both a nuisance (when flown too close to international airports, for instance) and an advance, especially within industries such as film-making and military surveillance. While I was never a fan of *Star Trek*, I'm aware of how their futuristic, flip-open communicators later became a reality with the advent of the mobile phone. At the time of the sci-fi classic's arrival in the mid-1960s a technology of that type was impossible to build, but the concept proved inspiring. Several decades later the smartphone became an innovation that went on to be possessed by millions of people. I can't deny that the world of comic-book superheroes is a hugely inspirational field when it comes to the question of what Gravity Industries might do next. Suspend any concern for production costs, material properties, investor returns or even the laws of physics and you have science fiction – a true distillation of human creativity. Who knows what might happen in one, five or ten years' time? We might be able to fly a rechargeable electric suit, or deploy wings to help us soar among the clouds even longer, higher and faster.

Of course, there will be people who say it can't be done, or that fantasizing about making the seemingly impossible possible is a waste of time. But historically, that attitude has been proved wrong time and time again. Take Bertha Benz, the wife of the German car designer Karl. In 1888, she drove her motor vehicle for 66 miles, a distance previously unimaginable. The journey was made unbeknown to her husband or the authorities, who probably would have deemed her road trip illegal. Up until that pivotal moment the car had only been driven for short distances and often with the help of a mechanic or two. But Bertha had thought, 'Sod that!' and she drove to her mother's house, proving to her husband that the motorcar possessed the potential for mass appeal. Her off-the-cuff decision arguably changed the world.

As with most innovations, it only took one person to alter the tide of opinion. The Californian community – to which Gravity Industries is very much connected – rarely crack a smile when making bold claims regarding our jet suit technology; they need little help to imagine we are on the cusp of a new era of human mobility. But if we're to alter public perception and devise a way in which we can develop the suit to be more convenient, affordable and mass production-ready, it's in the Gravity Industries workshop that those steps will take place. After all, it's from this development lab that the current components of the suit have been created and fine-tuned. Let me talk you through the inventory...

The engines

The way in which I built the suit was to take an existing problem and solve it. The challenge was this: if a person weighed 75 kilos, as I did, how could I logically create enough propulsion to push down with 75 kilos of force? If I was to manage that feat I'd effectively become weightless. Beyond that, if I were able to create a downward force of 76 kilos, I'd generate 1 kilo of thrust and therefore the potential for flight.

I knew there were engines with the capacity to create that level of power. But where exactly would I put them on my body? The immediate answer was found in the arms and legs because they have naturally evolved to take weight. Human limbs are also very controllable. So I placed two engines on each arm in a handheld assembly and an engine on each leg, creating a triangulated area of thrust that pushed the jet suit wearer upwards.

That was the theory, anyway.

Our legs are designed to press against a hard surface. When we bend at the knees, even slightly (as tends to happen during take-off, as the brain wrestles with the uncomfortable concept of taking flight in a jet suit throwing out over 1,000 horsepower), the engines attached to the calves can easily deviate from vertical and propel you in unwanted directions. Many attempts to fly the suit in that way ended up with me spinning around in circles as I fought to control my legs.

There were other technical problems with attaching two engines to my legs. The heat created by my handheld turbines would sometimes be ingested by the lower engines, increasing their own exhaust temperature beyond the melting point of steel, resulting in the blades disappearing in a puff of sparks. On other occasions, the thrust from the leg engines destroyed the ground below, blowing debris back up into the engines, damaging their internal workings. Despite achieving the first breakthrough flight with this arrangement, somehow mastering the required balance, I eventually opted to move the leg engines up to my lower back, which created a stable wigwam of thrust – a web of power formed by the turbines mounted on each arm and on my back.

Since the early testing sessions in 2016 there have been a number of evolutions in the placement of the mini jet turbines, and, looking back, some of those early incarnations were very unreliable and unstable. Weirdly, though, in clutch situations, where I've had to perform on request, they rarely let me down. I remember appearing on *The One Show* on the BBC in 2017, where I was told that I'd have to start the system live and fly on command. Cameras rolling, I became increasingly uncomfortable as my engines came up to idle slowly, fearing my reputation was about to shatter in front of an audience of millions. One of my rear turbines flamed dramatically and lagged the other five that were all showing a readiness to accelerate.

'Oh God,' I thought. 'This is not going well.'

Miraculously, after what seemed like an age the final green light pinged on, indicating the sixth turbine had made it, and my focus switched to not falling over in front of the presenters, Matt Baker and Alex Jones. Given the restrictions of what I was able to do with the suit at that time, not to mention the decision to live-stream my ninety-second start-up process, I'm sure there were one or two underwhelmed viewers at home. In those early days, flying fairly low to the ground was my choice purely on the grounds of safety, and we hadn't even tried to test the suit's capabilities. A few online commentators asserted that we were entirely dependent on 'ground effect' and couldn't fly any higher, but the opposite has always been true: ground effect typically involves flying along with a compressed cushion of air between a wing and the ground, but we don't use a wing and flying close to the ground actually allows the hot exhaust to recirculate back into the engines resulting in a loss of power.

The handheld engine assemblies have gone through a variety of designs and materials. The first ones were crafted from scratch using aluminium tubes, drilled over a hundred times to reduce weight. They're now constructed from a mixture of aluminium and polymer 3D custom-printed parts. I've always attached the engines to my arms because I liked the idea of moving the thrust around naturally, with limbs and natural human balance, rather than a jet suit that altered direction via expensive, movable ducts in a backpack system. We've also kept the number of fallible components to a minimum, and ensured a failure event can only ever result in a descent rather than an uncontrolled altitude gain. I tried a large number of positions when learning how best to attach the engines, and I soon found that one on each side of both arms, fore and aft, was the most effective. In that position, the net thrust felt as if it was a part of the body and became very easy to control.

Meanwhile, I realized that relying on basic physics was the best way of controlling directional thrust as I flew through the air. I could have designed a system that altered the altitude and flight trajectory of the suit by accelerating each individual engine, and the very first flights were achieved with one throttle control for the arms and one for the legs, but even that left me feeling as if I was playing the piano rather than manoeuvring naturally like a gymnast or a skateboarder. Practically speaking, it's also hard to spool these engines up and down finely enough to balance in that manner. Then I realized that if you break down the thrust across the whole suit and plot the components on a graph, it is possible to create extremely precise changes by simply moving your arms. It was really a question of using my brain. If I felt I was moving too far to the right, I adjusted the direction of thrust with my arms. It became obvious that a lot of these behaviours were second nature already, as they are when a person is skiing, or riding a bike.

The thrust and the weight of the arm engines are what cause the most physical load during flight. When walking around, fully suited up, it's the heavy equipment. With a full tank, everything weighs around 35 kilos, which isn't too dissimilar to the weight carried by Royal Marines Commandos as they yomp around with their webbing, weapon, Bergen and other equipment. That type of physical burden can soon wear a person down when they walk. In the same way that a penguin is designed to move smoothly in the water but is rather ungainly on land, so the suit is designed to be in the air. Still very compact for something with more power than an F1 car, just not much to hang around in for long stretches of time. Until the engines lift themselves, that is, when the experience becomes elegant, tuned and graceful.

During the early days of flight, I was sometimes uncomfortable when staying in the air for too long, especially when burning through a lot of fuel. The lighter the fuel tanks became, the more I'd have to vector my arms out to the sides in order to shed thrust. (Removing my finger from the throttle isn't sensitive enough; you have around 1,000 bhp over less than 10mm of throttle travel.) That meant I sometimes ended up in a crucifix position towards the end of a flight, my arms almost level with the shoulders as I held out 6 kilos of micro jet turbine on each side, the lactic acid burning through my muscles, turbulence buffeting my body. In the early phases of testing there was nothing more unnerving than feeling the scorching tremble of muscular failure while flying 300 metres away from the shoreline of a lake, which I often flew over for safety reasons – water is much more forgiving than concrete during a crash landing. I'd have no choice but to grit my teeth through the agony and head for land as quickly as possible.

These days we have computer code integrated with the engines, which turns the power down as the suit burns through its fuel. This allows me to fly with my arms by my sides at all times. We have refined so much of the suit geometry and flight set-up that during a busy day of filming, or testing, I sometimes feel like it's possible to soar around all day.

The helmet

At first, I used any protective equipment that was built for the extreme sports arena: ski and snowboard helmets were bought, sometimes mountain bike body armour. For a while I even used the type of racing helmet worn by the Olympic cyclist Chris Hoy – super-lightweight and aerodynamic, it came with a visor and looked suitably purposeful. These days we use a very lightweight carbon helmet, with a Sony SmartEyeglass heads-up display system, though we've used a number of different manufacturers. This technology acts as a dashboard and projects all the vital data I need to know on to the inside of my visor. As I fly, I simply glance to check my speed, fuel, engine data and flight time. The last statistic is useful because my fuel data has been known to fail sometimes. I always know how much airtime I'm carrying in the tank, however, so I'll instead lean on my flight time in order to gauge when I need to prepare for a landing.

There's quite a lot of information to take in when I'm flying. Currently, the speed is measured by GPS data on an Android phone strapped to my leg that then feeds the heads-up display. It's not the most accurate thing in the world, but it's a good indication, and it's an app we've had specially designed. Android phones are lightweight, with a big screen and a very long battery life; they are relatively cheap and use a language that is simple to code and process. All of this is so much better than the early days, when I'd have to glance down at the electronics system on my chest to check the status of each engine (and safer than my first version of the suit, which comprised some wiring stuffed into a Tupperware box). Often I'd only realize something was wrong when a light or two flashed, alerting me that one of the engines hadn't started up properly, usually just as I was about to take off. Most embarrassingly, I flew a good two dozen events with my wife's old pink iPhone hastily shoved into my boot just before take-off, the vibration alert set to two minutes as an early warning that I should be bringing my display to a close. I rarely felt it buzzing away, but as a physical comfort placebo it was invaluable.

Fuel tanks

I started out buying 300-litre drums of paraffin, but now we use proper Jet A-1 aviation fuel of the type used in civilian and military jets, which is actually pretty benign and hard to ignite. When it does, there's a very lazy flame, the kind you might see on a Christmas pudding or flaming Sambuca, which slowly builds to give off an intense heat. Having said that, fire must be respected and we have a pair of extinguishers on hand at all times, just in case, although I'm pleased to say we've never had cause to use one. We also make sure to fly wearing flame-resistant Nomex or merino wool underlayers, avoiding most synthetic materials that could easily burn or melt should things go wrong. But the risk is surprisingly low; I certainly have no sensation of heat unless flying in a very confined space, where the hot exhaust doesn't have much chance to dissipate.

There was quite a creative process behind the fuel bladders we currently use with the suit. Located on the backpack, by the rear engine, and fed to all five turbines by an effective tubing network, we have a system that evolved from an adapted waterproof rucksack-style liner, otherwise known as a canoe bag. The latest jet suits now use a pair of custom-welded polyurethane fuel bladders, but the principles are exactly the same. The tanks are squidgy to the touch and, as the jet fuel is consumed, the bags remain airtight and compact, meaning that the liquid inside doesn't slosh about or escape. Without equipment of that kind, were I to take a corner at high speed, all the fuel would move around, risking any contained air interrupting the flow of fuel to the engines, very likely shutting them down, which is an event best avoided.

During the early development phases I used camping gear to feed fuel into the engines – polyurethane, pill-shaped canvas bags that mountaineers filled with water for drinking; alternatively, they could be hung, filled with around 10 litres of water and fitted with a shower head for washing. During the early stages of the design I had one of these dromedary bags fitted on each side of the suit's backpack.

My guiding principle when designing the suit has always been to take the magpie approach to design: if somebody has already spent time and money making a robust, existing product that nearly fits all our design requirements, why not use it until we've learned exactly what does and doesn't work?

The electronics control system

This is primarily in place to take the pilot's simple control inputs and start, accelerate and shut down the turbines, via something called pulse width modulation. I've designed it so that the vital components are always visible, in case the heads-up display doesn't work for any reason, or if I'm flying without it: I only have to glance down to see that the batteries and their connections are working on a glowing electronics panel and a series of illuminated interrogation ports. If something goes wrong I can usually tell immediately. The flashing lights deliver a cinematic element too: from a distance the gadgetry of the early suit resembled Darth Vader's breastplate.

Some thought went into how much of the electrical system should be on display. Did I really want to clad myself in so much technology that I became more machine than person? Or did I want to hide all the technology in one big backpack? In which case there was a risk I'd have been regarded as some bloke in a leather jacket with a big pack on and two strange contraptions attached to my arms. Having the electronics up front pushed me halfway there. The look physically represented human being and technology working together, which was the whole point all along.

The electronics control system is housed in what looks like a waist-coat, a custom CAD design, 3D-printed in polymer, which has evolved over at least fifty iterations and clips across the front of the pilot. The entire set-up is designed to be modular.

Having been through so much research and development, all of this technology is now custom-made and tightly integrated within the suit in such a way as to minimize the risk of failure. In the early days of prototyping so many electrical connectors were prone to moving position, which was nightmarish, especially mid-flight. If a wire or two broke loose and severed a connection even momentarily, it might shut down an individual engine. It soon became imperative to eliminate any movement and tension between cables and connectors. I have way too many electrical devices at home that go a bit 'blinky' the minute a cable is pinched, or knocked out of place, which is fine when it's a flaky iPhone charger; it's not so fine when travelling at 75 km/h over a Formula One racetrack.

The entire suit is designed with stability and reliability in mind. I don't enjoy stress. I like calm and relaxed. And despite the fact I might look like a daredevil as I'm soaring around at high speeds, the jet suit is very much designed to be as safe as we can possibly make it.

Snake-proof footwear

These days I wear a light and sturdy pair of motorbike boots, but throughout much of 2017 quite a fuss was made of the fact that I was using knee-high, snake-proof footwear during air shows and displays. There was some logic behind their inclusion, however. Having tested variations of engine placements at the farm, it became clear that with so much hot air flying around, particularly when I was standing on concrete, my feet and lower legs would get rather warm. In the very early development phases, when I had a turbine attached to each leg, the heat reflecting back off the ground was a constant battle and would steadily melt even the soles of my modified motocross boots. At one point, my wife had to stuff a running water hose into the top of my boots to cool my very hot feet.

Intent on fending off the problem, even with the turbines now affixed to my lower back, I typed the words 'boot', 'heatproof' and 'knee high' into Google and sat back to wade through all manner of racy leather and stiletto-based footwear, until eventually I stumbled upon a small range of boots typically intended for Texan rangers and hikers who apparently had to deal with aggressive rattlesnake attacks when walking in the high desert. The footwear wasn't intended to be heat-resistant but was made from a lightweight canvas construction reinforced with bite-proof Kevlar and plentiful padding to frustrate even the most determined snake. I shipped them in from America and used them for quite a while, much to the amusement of anyone writing about my work. We eventually stopped using them after we moved to the single rear engine, which directed the heat away from the legs.

Workshop Notes

CREATE A GREEN SCREEN
FOR YOUR AUDIENCE

I could have emerged from my R&D phase with a jet suit that looked otherworldly, like something from a DC Comics strip, or a *Flash Gordon* TV series. And in a small way I guess the commonly drawn parallel with fictional characters like Bruce Wayne or Tony Stark is not without some reasoning: in my spare time I've developed a suit from my man cave that allows me to fly. Though I'm at pains to point out that I'm not a billionaire and didn't embark on this journey with any designs to become the next Batman.

Had I projected that idea on to my suit with garish colours or a lightning bolt logo, I might have suffered an embarrassing reception. Audiences watching me as I flew around could have been underwhelmed. I would have run a high risk of being derided for my efforts because visually it's impossible to recreate all the manoeuvres and stunts pulled off by the characters in a multi-million-dollar superhero movie.

Instead, with a bit of guidance from a small circle of those I trust, we went for a mostly black, rather reserved look because that created a blank canvas for audiences upon which to paint their own ideas, like a Hollywood green screen where CGI effects are added around the actors during post-production. Somebody could watch my flight and picture the wearer as a James Bond-style operator. Someone else might simply see a new form of transport. Another person might indeed see the real-life manifestation of their Marvel hero.

This neutral presentation is effective because when an eyewitness applies imagination to a technological leap such as a jet suit, *they own that leap.* They later describe it in excited terms to the people they talk to, because they've added a personal idea to something they have witnessed. In effect, they sell the idea to other people, not me. Had I set myself or Gravity up with claims of fulfilling some science-fiction superhero fantasy, then I would have been easily pigeonholed, and more open to criticism.

I think this is something we can apply to all forms of innovation. We have ideas and we can choose to frame those ideas specifically, to the tiniest detail. We might have designed an exclusive app that helps big city accountants to estimate a client's annual tax bills on a daily basis. But why frame that product in a way that only targets big city accountants when we can make the concept a little ambiguous so that small business owners, freelancers or people running a part-time industry from home can picture themselves using it too? Allowing others to imagine what our product can be used for is easier and more fun than setting defined boundaries. It makes good commercial sense, too.

Takeaways

○ Science fiction and fantasy is a source of inspiration when working in technology and engineering. Some of the ideas of the future will emerge from the CGI effects on our cinema screens, and Hollywood has been an excellent source of new ideas. The flip phone (*Star Trek*) and driverless car (*Total Recall*) were originally conceived in film and TV before they were designed for real.

○ We should surround ourselves with the things that have inspired us, as I've done with the Harrier and Sea King components hanging in my workshop. When the work seems tough, it's good to have a reminder of why we started along a particular path in the first place.

○ Take the magpie approach to research and development. Don't spend silly money and time commissioning perfection. Instead, find something that does the job just as well, or at least 70 per cent as effectively, and then road-test it. Learn, adapt and then settle on what is worth pursuing before you order a custom-built version.

○ When launching a new idea or concept, it sometimes works not to force its purpose down the throats of others. Let them imagine the possibilities of a new idea and take emotional ownership of its potential.

TEAM BUILDING

Or, How to Stress-test Your Relationships

t's vital the teams we work with bring the same enthusiasm to a project as we do. A start-up requires people with a shared energy and vision – that spirit can sometimes be the force that carries an idea or innovation over the line.

Since we launched Gravity in April 2017 thousands of people have contacted us, seeking out employment or experience. At the time of writing I still manage to personally reply to the vast majority, and those interactions often produce the most interesting and diverse insights. But only those with a highly unusual degree of drive, creativity, and a willingness to go many extra miles, have formed the team around me. We have people who first and foremost are collaborating with us for the joy of the challenge, the thrill of being part of something special, in an environment where boundless thought and hands-on creativity is encouraged.

As entrepreneurs or creative leaders, when looking to expand our teams it's vital to look for those flawed but passionate and skilled candidates rather than the safer choices. The unpolished diamond might not necessarily seem like the best person on paper at first, but usually they end up being a better choice than a super-experienced candidate who treats the role as a nine-to-five gig, or someone solely in it for the money. Those individuals are unlikely to muck in when the going gets rough, or to deliver an unobvious idea or unconventional plan.

As with most business decisions, however, there's no exact science to making the right call. Choices like these are often based on educated hunches. We have to trust our gut. I know I have when picking some of the people I've brought into the fold, and one of these figures was Angelo Grubisic, aka Pilot #002 at Gravity

Industries, who was a world-class skydiver. He had plans to fly 'higher, faster and further' than any human has done before, unaided by a craft, by leaping from a plane at an altitude of 40,000 feet, the highest ever jump of that kind. Sadly, Angelo passed away during the writing of this book in a terrible accident in Saudi Arabia, but we are all blessed and grateful to have known and spent time with such an exceptional person.

Angelo wasn't a brainless speed demon with an inability to register fear, he adored wing-suiting and was a highly educated enthusiast. In fact his full title was Dr Angelo Grubisic, and when he wasn't flying around in the jet suit, or in a wingsuit preparing for the record-breaking project-in-waiting, entitled The Icarus Project, he could be found working at his full-time job as a lecturer in Astronautics and Advance Propulsion within Engineering and Physical Sciences at Southampton University. Still, tragedy underpinned his high-speed endeavours. He lost his life in 2019 whilst wing-suiting in Saudi Arabia, months after having been crowned British National Wingsuit Champion. He died doing something he loved, and in response to the question of taking up a crazy, dangerous hobby, he would often say, 'If you're not doing what you love, then you're the crazy one.'

Despite what people might think, the jet suit, for me, is not about being brave, crazy or courageous. I've deliberately reined in the full capacity of the suit, having run an exhaustive series of risk assessments. So far the highest speeds, altitudes and times travelled run as follows: 85 km/h; 8 metres or so – but there's nothing to stop us from going thousands of feet into the air; and two minutes.

Theoretically, one day in a fit of pique I might think, 'Oh, sod it, let's just go to a thousand feet and buzz Old Sarum Airfield in Salisbury.' But I know that's never going to happen, because I don't have any serious inclination to do it. There is literally no upside. Plus, our displays are best viewed when I am low. If I was too high, I would be a speck in the sky. It makes sense to fly low and stick close to my support crew, easily stopping to check equipment and fuel before flying off again.

Building, flying and testing prototype jet suits is vastly different to Angelo's world of wing-suiting, which, at its highest level, becomes a test of nerve for those remarkable people willing to accept the devastating risk or subsequent rewards of completing each flight. I hugely valued Angelo's passion and enthusiasm, and having him as part of our team helped everyone push forward to really appreciate the joy and thrill of flight.

How I came to work with someone with such an exuberant personality is an interesting story in its own right and an example of why picking passionate people to operate alongside is always the best choice. As the suit's development progressed, there were exhibitions and displays to attend, more creative opportunities to attack and a highly managed brand expansion in place. It became obvious that my support staff had to grow alongside Gravity Industries. I brought in a PR company to help with media and events. And I have been lucky enough to be surrounded by excellent collaborators and volunteers who have supported with the designing and engineering aspects of the suit, as well as helping at events. But there came a point when I realized a second pilot was needed, partly to add an extra wow factor to the air shows and demonstrations we were increasingly performing, but also to bring a different perspective to the workings of the suit – and prove to the world that others could learn to fly it.

Which is where Angelo came in.

In 2017 I was invited to appear on children's television for the BBC, a commitment I fulfilled in a very jetlagged state. Having met the presenter, Andy, an ex-military freefaller, I set about delivering the flight display in front of the cameras. The general gist of his programme was to showcase various processes in the natural world while explaining how a bloke like him might recreate those feats. Andy wanted to see if, with the aid of micro turbines, he could theoretically accelerate his normal freefall to match the 230 mph speed of a peregrine falcon in full stoop. My role in all of this was to arrive at a location in Wiltshire, fly in, land and shake hands with Andy, and reveal the workings of the jet suit as part of his presentation. It all seemed like a bit of fun, and perfectly in line with what Gravity was doing as a brand, specifically supporting our STEM agenda.

When I arrived, I noticed that a tall blond bloke with long surfer-dude hair was standing near by. He was introduced as Dr Angelo Grubisic. Angelo then mentioned something about being a wingsuit pilot, and alerted me to his fascination with jet engines. My mind was in a jetlagged daze, my only priority to deliver the flight and piece to camera. But after I'd executed a successful flight, Angelo seemed keen to get to know me better.

'It would be great to catch up and talk about the suit some time,' he said.

It was a suggestion I'd heard countless times previously from various individuals, and one that rarely generated a follow-up conversation. A lot of the time people gave me their details and then failed to deliver on what they had proposed or volunteered, so my expectations were set relatively low. I think we exchanged details but both dived back into our busy lives and neglected to follow up.

And then fate played its hand.

In a world where every technological advance seems to carry a military potential, I was invited to the Johns Hopkins University in Maryland, USA, where I'd been asked to deliver a talk and flight demo to various Navy SEALs chiefs and a group of military technologists specializing in all things secret and cutting-edge. The idea was for my presentation to shake up military minds about what was possible with the jet suit from a defence perspective. Among the presentation team was the chief test pilot and co-designer of the *Squirrel* wingsuit, Matt Gerdes – a lively American with over 1,200 jumps to his name. And alongside him was . . . Angelo. Apparently he was collaborating with Matt on the design and wind tunnel testing of a pioneering wingsuit.

'OK, fate really is trying to work hard here to get us together,' I thought.

Angelo was just as enthusiastic as when we had met a few months previously. 'I've been flying in wingsuits,' he told me. 'I'm a lecturer in aeronautics. And I've now decided my next goal in life is to experience flight in your jet suit. I think it's the most awesome thing in the world. I want to be a pilot. What do I have to do?'

I was sold. Before long Angelo was testing out the suit at Gravity Industries, and what became apparent very quickly was that his prior experience was immensely helpful when it came to understanding the physics of the challenge. After three or four sessions, during which he grasped the mechanics of the suit while attached to a safety tether, Angelo was flying around unleashed. It was a big moment for me. So many people had scoffed at my plans to teach others to fly, and quickly. The general feeling was that it was simply too hard to prepare new pilots; many people thought that picking up the required techniques and experience wasn't dissimilar to learning how to pilot a helicopter. In the early days the suit was very physical, so there was also a misconception that the strain from the 1,000-horsepower engines would be too much on the average person's arms. My thinking was different. Mastering the jet suit was more in the realm of learning to ski or snowboard. The only thing required was a slight readjustment in thinking, as the body and brain rewired themselves in order to handle the unusual physics of flying in a jet suit. Angelo had proved my theorizing correct and Pilot #002 was soon installed in Gravity's line-up.

To say he was chuffed was an understatement and we began working together quite quickly. The very first dual flight was fittingly at the Farnborough Airshow in July 2018. Then in August we really upped the ante and staged a series of boundary-pushing displays at the Bournemouth Air Festival. Over a blisteringly hot weekend, Angelo and I conducted a series of flights, taking off from the famous pier as crowds of people gathered on the beach below. Despite the physical risks associated with flying a jet suit, I rarely spend time thinking about crashing because I take so much care with regard to pre-flight checks and watching my speed and altitude during flights; I tend to check and then recheck the jet suit over and over in the build-up to a performance. I regard my particular mode of transport as being not too dissimilar to riding a motorbike in terms of the dangers involved; I'd imagine with snowboarding and skiing there's a higher chance of serious injury. But when we both stepped towards the edge of the pier the day before our flight, the waves lapping several metres below us, I became a little tense.

'Oh, this is a bit high,' I thought, laughing nervously. 'I don't really like heights.'

To my surprise, Angelo later admitted to sharing my unease. That might have seemed like a strange admission, coming from somebody who BASE jumps off Alpine cliffs in wingsuits in his spare time, but I understood his disassociation from fear when in the zone. Once Angelo has his suit on, there is a job to do. He trusts in his equipment and he understands there is a risk he might crash, but he still feels confident enough to press ahead; he understands the science and has decided not to worry. However, while standing near to a cliff edge or on top of a high building without his kit, he feels as exposed as the rest of us. I feel the same way about the jet suit. Without the suit on, surveying a flight can be daunting. Once I have the equipment on and the engines running, those fears usually fade away.

The slight edginess we experienced on Bournemouth Pier was worth it. Angelo set a speed of 46 mph, a then unofficial world record. I set a new distance benchmark at 1.4 km. Knowing we were over water, wearing life jackets, and with an escort of jet-skiing lifeguards, we did push hard, knowingly entertaining more risk than usual. Seeing us both have separate spills into the sea at various stages wasn't what I had in mind, but it taught us a lot. As ever, we've always learned more from our mistakes than when everything goes to plan.

The night after Angelo's dramatic swim, as we hosed down his damage suit, we discovered that he always carried two items in the back pocket of his flight trousers. The first was a sew-on flight badge previously worn by his grandfather, which had confirmed him as one of the earliest wingsuit pilots on record. The second was no less than three different-coloured Sharpie pens, including a gold one, to sign those all-important autographs for fans.

Like I said earlier: passion is everything.

Workshop Notes

BUILD THE RIGHT TEAM AROUND YOU

Something that has sadly become rare in corporate culture is passion for the final product. People are compartmentalized; they're told what to do, which really only encourages them to focus on a small area of the process. They don't feel as passionate or have any real ownership over the bigger picture, so if something doesn't work they don't feel the frustration as keenly as someone who has invested in the concept as a whole. It's the same with success: they don't typically get to enjoy the upside either.

At Gravity Industries I've tried to create a culture where everybody involved is responsible for their domain; they do everything they can to deliver, but they're also encouraged to step up and take care of any issues involving the bigger picture. At air shows we have had people working on a display stand, helping the public enjoy our VR flight experience and answering questions about the jet suit. But they might approach me to say,

'Actually, what about doing this on the flight?' Or, 'I have an idea for a publicity opportunity.'

This is a breath of fresh air, especially when compared to working in a big corporation where employees are rarely encouraged or permitted to look beyond their immediate departments. It ensures that everybody pulls in the right direction, and with enthusiasm.

As Gravity Industries expanded in size and stature throughout 2018, appearance offers from around the globe began to come in on a daily basis. We went to Farnborough Airshow, where I was asked to fly in the same programme as the latest civil airliners and top-end jet fighters. We even had a conversation with a Spanish Air Force Harrier pilot that resulted in one of my favourite photos, with him hovering his Harrier in the background as I hang suspended in the jet suit at the front of the shot. My late grandfather on my mother's side had been the CEO and chairman at Westland Helicopters UK, and conducted deals worth tens of millions of pounds from that same airfield; he was one of the big names at Farnborough for years, a location that calls itself 'The Home of Aviation'. And there I was, his grandson, showcasing a new development in human aviation on the same runway. The pressure not to succumb to engine failure mid-flight was huge.

I then flew to Bentonville in America, where I conducted a successful flight demonstration despite the fact that seawater from Angelo's tumble at Bournemouth had damaged the kill switch on the arm-mounted engines, meaning I had to solder the wires together in order to fly smoothly. Nobody noticed.

This little merry-go-round was probably one of the most intense and stressful, and then relieving and validating, ten days of my life. Throughout 2017 and 2018 we dashed all over the world, the jet suit in a pair of check-in suitcases, delivering display after display. It was seriously hard work but immensely rewarding. I was building an audience. I was making connections with powerful people involved in interesting companies within a variety of industries. Most of all, every event acted like a polling station, where I could gauge the public reaction to my work almost immediately.

'This is real,' I thought. 'This is so much better than sitting back at home, watching web traffic statistics. This feels like a serious brand now.'

But not everybody was as enthusiastic about my whirlwind lifestyle. My family life was beginning to crack under the pressure.

When my work began on building the jet suit in 2016, Debbie must have wondered what was happening to the person she'd married all those years earlier, as my new career lurched forward and created a fair deal of disruption. From March to November of that year I embarked on a journey that involved plenty of sleep deprivation while figuring out how best to build a suit that allowed me to fly. That was fun. The period between December and April 2017 was an entirely different challenge. I became anxious of where my work might take me financially and emotionally; the tension within the family seemed stretched to breaking point. It was as if I'd become a different person: a man masquerading in a secure and well-paid job in the City while designing a jet suit. In the process I'd detached myself from the family and left Debbie to look after our kids as I single-mindedly set out to realize my ambition.

Debbie, at that point, would have been well within her rights to ask some serious questions of me. Among them would have been the following:

What's it for?

Why is this so important to you?

Instead she left me to it, but her doubts were palpable. In reaction, I closed down, shutting myself away amid the whirlwind of work. I had my own doubts and knew I had to be selective about who I ushered into my fragile new world. I wanted to be surrounded by enthusiasm; I needed an all-guns-blazing attitude about me.

'I'm going to fuel myself through this journey by believing I've genuinely achieved something significant here,' I told myself.

Later on in 2017, and in 2018, the bigger the company became the less time I was able to spend at home with Debbie and the kids. My desire for success, both on the business side and in terms of the development of the suit itself, had become consuming. To make matters worse, I was forever being distracted by revenue-generating events, interview requests and public appearances. Whenever I made a conscious effort to spend some time in the UK an opportunity would arise that meant travelling to China to deliver a presentation on the suit, or some other country to do a talk for a room of high-powered businesspeople. The workload was utterly disorientating. It was, unsurprisingly, rough on Debbie.

If I wasn't working away on the other side of the world in my new role – with the added worry that my flights went smoothly – I was recovering from jetlag, or catching up with R&D in the workshop. I was often distracted and distant. Matters were worse when I was abroad because we could only communicate online, or during a phone call, which only increased the tension. Debbie, understandably, was frustrated and upset. I know she was nervous about where the project was taking me and worried about the person I was becoming, especially as I was moving into some quite unexpected circles. Not being able to share this journey entirely with Debbie was hard, as she invariably had to stay at home to look after our kids and pets while I ventured into the world of media and TV interviews, and globe-trotted my way around in order to promote Gravity and generate some income.

The kids were probably just as unsettled by my unpredictable presence at home. It's easy to assume that our children will fall in love with whatever wild or far-out projects we might become involved with. Rock-star kids should love rock music. The children of footballers should enjoy watching and playing football. And the sons of a jet suit designer should revel in the fact that their dad can fly around the world with his invention. It's definitely the case that my boys are proud of what we have built, and never more so than when I have flown and spoken at their schools. But it's also true that they recognize the business inevitably competes with them for my time. As the boys have got older they have been able to get involved in some parts of the company, which is great fun for all of us, but there is no doubt being a father and an entrepreneur is a challenge.

Matters haven't been helped by the fact that I also tend to be rather restless. I'm afflicted by a very Western urge to move forward, to progress, no matter what is going on around me. My attitude towards any success has been to think, 'Done that, now what?' It moved me through university, military life and then my oil-trading career. I was in a hurry to get on with everything. At BP I didn't want to look back and reflect on my successes, nor did I wish to stand still. Embracing the present moment was an almost impossible concept to me, which was probably why when I tried them I found the practices of yoga and mindfulness to be difficult to subscribe to. I was forever wondering about the next deadline or target as I attempted to settle my breath and silence my inner critic.

Anyone who feels a passion for work can become consumed by a project or process. Ideas and pressures swamp our thinking; days and then nights are taken up with tasks until they become our sole focus. Everything else seems like an unwelcome distraction, even the things that bring richness to our lives, such as our friends and family. Yet these hugely important connections nourish us when moving towards a goal or deadline, and are vital when we come down from whatever temporary high we may be experiencing. Family members and friends provide support networks and release valves. We shouldn't neglect them.

For a more detailed analysis, I've asked Debbie to describe the experience of sharing a life with a fidgety, over-worked designer hell-bent on turning the family home into a makeshift laboratory. This is her version of events . . .

When I first saw Richard powering up a micro turbine in our garage, I was really quite excited. The waft of jet fuel

Left: The young Michael Browning, my father.

Above: The two of us together when I was a small boy, sitting in an aircraft. We were passionate . . .

Above: A cobbled-together sail boat – one of the creations I hacked together out of scraps in my father's workshop.

Above: A humorous present my father received when leaving Westlands. This picture sits in our lab now and, despite the stern passport photo, nicely reflects his flight and engineering passions at the time.

Left: Flying model radio-controlled gliders with my father in Dorset.

Above left: The London Royal Marines Reserve Unit, at the end of Phase One Bravo at Lympstone.

Above right: Debbie and I at a BP Gala dinner in the City of London.

Remote paddling and wild camping in Canada with Debbie and the boys. We've always encouraged a sense of adventure.

Left: The original engine test-bed: an old washing machine which required the tether to an old heavy go-kart to prevent it from tipping over.

Below: The first turbine laid out on the lounge floor . . . manual open!

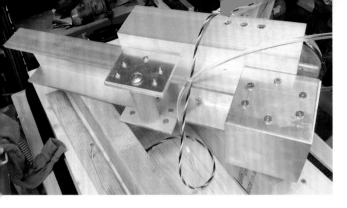

Left: The Mark One arm engine mount. Hugely overbuilt as a reflection of my concern for what it would be like to hold on to a jet engine!

Below: The Mark Two arm engine mount - a pair of aluminium tubes modified to house an engine and my arm.

Right: The Mark Two arm engine mount, with many holes drilled in it in an effort to relentlessly chase down weight.

Below: The very first engine test standing in a lane in the UK with that experimental arm mount and learning that it was eminently controllable.

Right: Competing for space on the kitchen table with Oliver doing his homework.

Below left: Oliver trying on one of the arm engine assemblies.

Below right: Thomas and Oliver in the converted bedroom we used in the early days for some of the engineering work.

Below: Fiddly electronics work in the first week Alex Wilson joined me in 2018.

Left: Two engines, one on each arm, as I jump around a field to get a feel for the thrust.

Below: Trying a turbine on each leg, one on each arm, and a rolling tether for safety. The latter proved unworkable.

Above: Relentless testing. This was a phase when we moved the leg engines to my posterior, and tried housing the electronics in a tupperware box on my back.

Left: Learning from failure. This is when we'd moved to a single rear engine. You can see the cowling squashed after a fall. Key to our ethos was making those failures as safe as possible, so it was only a few feet.

Above: Learning to fly the hard way by bounding around and giving myself moments in the air to try and learn how to balance with thrust on each leg and each arm.

Right: That very first six-second controlled flight in October 2016; and landing it! That was the moment when I realized it was genuinely possible and this was just the beginning.

was thrilling, the noise was unbelievable (and far too loud!), and to see his enthusiasm was brilliant. I didn't see it as him having a mid-life crisis. Rather it was an extension of the innovation work he was doing with BP (before being frustrated by the corporate nature of a company of that size) and the mad things he used to do with our boys at the weekends, such as melting copper and aluminium in a homemade furnace. He's always been a daredevil father, up for taking the boys to do something practical and visceral, and the eccentricity of the suit was brilliant.

But as it became more serious, as the suit gathered lots of attention, I found it harder to understand what the work meant and where it might be heading. As it came to dominate our lives more and more, it was difficult to fathom what was going on. My mum and I worry during every single event or test that Richard might have an accident, get hurt or perhaps burned. What would happen then? Would he carry on? Probably!

In the early stages I'd become tired sometimes when we'd spend a weekend clearing away mud from the barn at a cattle farm he used to work from – if we didn't, it tended to fly up into the engines, which then caused all sorts of problems – but I was happy to help. I didn't mind his late-night work, or the fact our spare room had been turned into a workshop. It was when he began to really take flight that the issues started. Red Bull and *Wired* magazine came to see the workshop and interviewed Richard, though he was still unsure whether there would be a global appeal for his idea at that time. But that wider attention was a turning point in his attitude. I was recovering from an operation back then and I was feeling like I needed some peace and stability.

Suddenly I was dealing with media interest and Richard launching a technology start-up. He wasn't grounded; there wasn't room for him to think about anything else and by distancing himself from our sons and me, Richard was unable to tap into the natural support network provided by a connected family unit.

The turning point came for Richard when he found a confidence in the team he was building around himself. By sharing his vision and finding such valuable support in the other members of Gravity he has been able to redress that very important balance between his working day and our home life.

As he went from strength to strength, it was brilliant to hear about what was going on. I was so proud when he did a TED Talk in 2017 and then flew the suit under serious pressure. I knew how much that meant to him. But I tended to feel a little bit helpless, because a lot of his events were taking place on the other side of the world. I didn't mind him being away too much; what I found hard was the idea he was going to places like China or America and experiencing a lot of big moments, but I wasn't there to share them with him. I'm the mother to two boys: I think that's the most important job in the world, but doing the same routines for ten years isn't as exciting as securing an investment deal for half a million pounds. At times his life sounded very glamorous (meeting celebrities, the super-rich, visiting amazing countries), whereas I was at home putting in the ninetieth washing load of the week and taking the kids on the school run. I know that might sound selfish, but I felt like I was no longer at the centre of his life, and that made it difficult to support what he was doing.

Marriage is about love, reliability, affection and stability. Entrepreneurship is almost the opposite of those things. It's about risk-taking, unpredictability, challenge and being a daredevil; the work is self-generated and it can focus on self-fulfilment. There's excitement all the time. But that life is very much the choice of the entrepreneur and I felt that Richard's work had been pushed upon the marriage. It hadn't been *our* idea, it was *his*, and I had to jump on for the crazy ride. That created the most tension. 'I can't *not* go along with it,' I thought. 'That would just drive us apart.'

Entrepreneurs like Richard are always moving forward. At BP he was constantly looking towards the next opportunity, and I often said to him, 'Be grateful and happy at what you've achieved. Look back and enjoy it.' I was always encouraging him to take a day off because he'd earned it. I feel the same way today. But Richard, like most successful creative people, has very high energy levels. He can't sit still. His brain works so hard all of the time: the jet suit and Gravity Industries are mapped out so well in his mind that he doesn't write anything down. Even when we go on a beach holiday we rarely relax with the other tourists. On one recent trip, rather than dozing on the sun loungers with everybody else, the family ventured to the opposite end of the beach where we built our own shelter from palm trees blown down in a storm and wood that had washed up on the beach. I loved it.

The problem with that focus and energy is that the family tends not to take centre stage. I often felt as if the kids and I lived in the shadow of his business and it became a challenge to ensure he stayed present when he was with us. I had to persuade him to wind down and relax. But I think we've found a nice rhythm in how we do things now. Richard listened when he could have shut down quite easily. I imagine a nagging wife must be something of an embuggerance to an innovative mind, caught in the thick of what can be seen as a ground-breaking project. But I wanted him to switch off for a while every week, to look up and realize there were other things going on in his life. The family were there to love and support him and to help give his busy brain a break. Some people might have stormed off to the pub in a mood at that point, but Richard gave me the time to explain my thoughts and feelings. He's realized that the early stages of his journey were a very hard time for us both; he's reflected back to me that he was in a difficult zone too, and that he'd lost sight of what was important. We can now understand that time together.

Today, I'm used to the level of work, and I am now finding my own path in all of this. From the beginning I was put in charge of the company's accounts and have assisted in countless events and test flights, all of which has helped me to feel more involved: I'm able to empathize with the stresses that take place at Gravity on a day-to-day level. I'm more connected. There have been difficult times, as there are for anyone embarking on an adventure such as this, but we've ridden it out fairly well. Yoga and keeping fit have helped me deal with any stress – I think spending more time on non-Gravity activities might benefit Richard too because switching off is really hard for him. But I'm so happy for everything he's achieved. We all feel excited for where his work might take him. Every time someone asks me what Richard has been up to, I'm always delighted to explain the latest developments, and as his wife I've loved championing his successes. I've also been on hand to provide Richard with the right levels of understanding and encouragement as he's made his innovative steps.

Behind any number of successful creative minds stands a partner willing to provide that extra layer of support, and I'm happy to take on that position within Richard's journey. We make a great team.

Workshop Notes

PERSONAL RELATIONSHIPS ARE OUR LIFE JACKET

Behind every person there's a successful partner and we need to remember they're not a distraction, or the enemy. When they ask us for quality time, it's because they love us, not because they want to take up our time for no reason.

The best way to be present in our relationships is to create strict windows of relaxation during which the work is put to one side – *no excuses*. This can be tricky, I know, especially when deadlines are looming, but take an hour or two every evening to have a meal together; turn off the phone and laptop and resist the urge to check emails and social media. Also, try to have meaningful conversations and discuss what's going on away from a project – people with an entrepreneurial spirit tend to be focused and serious about what they're doing, which sometimes leads to anxiety. Involve yourself in something fun that transports the focus away from work.

Debbie and I have discovered that sharing a household activity together can be very beneficial, such as painting a room, or tackling the garden. Not only are you achieving a task, but that style of work forces us to be mindful, to focus on the now. There's also space to talk and be together. This often acts as an excellent pressure valve, one that can help a couple to discuss and negotiate any tricky situations, or issues, before they escalate into a serious dispute.

Takeaways

○ When building a team, recruit a pool of diverse individuals packed with enthusiasm and passion, as well as experience, probably in that order. These are the attributes that can lead a project to success.

○ Stress-test relationships. Always check in with partners and loved ones for their feelings regarding our work. Family is the most important resource we have for love, support and understanding – and it's a two-way process. Don't neglect it.

○ Find a window every day to talk and share time with the people who are most important to us. Not only will it make them feel valued in those times when our focus is trained on an important project, but time spent away from work acts as an excellent stress release.

4

THE JUVENILE MIND

Or, How Thinking Like a Kid Can
Unlock True Innovation

row up.

It's the lesson issued to kids as soon as they begin acting like brats. The suggestion is that thinking sensibly, or maturely, represents the only path to proper adulthood, which is correct when teaching someone the social cues and patterns of acceptable behaviour required in the real world. The problem is this: being like a kid is at the very heart of innovative thinking. When most of the grown-ups in the room dismiss a concept or left-field thought as being too hard, or too silly, the childlike mind instead asks 'What if?' or, 'How about?' Often, exploring the possibilities deemed too ridiculous by a serious thinker becomes the gateway to a radical new idea.

I've noticed the power of childish thought in my own children as they play on computer games such as *Minecraft* – a building block programme that allows users to design all sorts of constructions in what is a wonderment of creation, and perfectly suited to the formative mind. I've often heard Oliver or one of his friends shouting out an idea excitedly. 'I know, let's build a moat!' they'll say. And then they're off, in a dreamland state, pondering how deep to make it, and where to position its drawbridge. But adults in that same situation would be more inclined to shrug their shoulders and announce that they've seen moats before, that they all look pretty much the same, and . . . 'So what?' That's because most grown-ups have become rubbish at tantalizing themselves with how amazing something might be. Their inclination to dream has been crushed by age; they give up at the first spark of an idea, fearful of it being deemed derivative, ludicrous or 'babyish'. Luckily, I wasn't one of those people.

How else do you think I came to build a jet suit?

Like a kid, I'm forever asking 'What if?' and 'Why don't we do this?' Which made me bloody annoying while I was at school, and later, when I worked for BP Oil, and most certainly during my time with the Royal Marines Reserve. Partly, my curiosity was a result of dyslexia, a condition that was spotted when I was very little and which meant communication, especially expressing myself via the written word, was a bit harder for me than it is for most people. I had to constantly raise my hand in class to ask questions because sitting through a lesson and later regurgitating on to paper what we'd learned was tough work. I was awful at English, or anything involving language or fact recall, and it was only really the visual subjects like Geography, Physics and Design and Technology that I found engaging.

Take Physics, for example. One approach to learning that particular science subject at school was to study various phenomena, such as what happened when a person threw an apple up in the air. Usually we learned the mathematical formulas that described a Granny Smith momentarily pausing in mid-air before accelerating downwards to meet the hand again. But there was an alternative for the dyslexic mind such as mine. I didn't necessarily have to learn the equations involved to understand their physics because I was able to visualize them logically. It made intuitive sense to me that when an apple is thrown into the air, its kinetic energy is rapidly eroded by the gravitational force until entirely converted into gravitational potential energy at its peak. At that point the apple pauses briefly, hanging suspended. This gravitational potential energy is then returned as ever-increasing kinetic energy, pulling the whole thing into reverse, which causes the apple to accelerate earthwards, where it then smacks back into the palm with the same level of energy it started out with. *Easy!*

Sadly, that intuitive understanding only got me so far during my school years. There were exams to pass, essays to write. I was told I had to memorize various scientific or mathematical relationships rather than explore them practically, and I was often asked to put my hand down despite having so many burning questions all of the time. It got to the point where my teachers didn't have the time or patience, or maybe even the knowledge, to explain my queries, or why the various calculus rules were the way they are. I must have been a pain in the arse a fair amount of the time.

I was the same way as a working professional. While at BP, I was thrown on to a trading desk and presented with a series of rules. At first, all of it was imparted in what sounded like an alien language, and I found it far easier to learn practically, in the field. Meanwhile, every snippet of information arrived too quickly for me to absorb because I wasn't one for simply accepting procedure. For every mention of a new rule, I became hung up on the intricacies of its meaning.

Every time a new function was revealed, my brain lit up with fifty supplemental questions. In training I often went off on tangents that were of no interest to anyone in the group but me. *Why is this? What about this? Surely this?* In the meantime the instructor had moved on to the next rule, leaving me floundering in a stew of confusion, my brain flipping through a Rolodex of possibilities. I was usually unafraid to look stupid, in the hope that my digging might unearth a legitimate question that nobody had ever thought of before.

As a kid, I realized that the process of education best suited to me was practical. I thrived when getting under the skin of something, and I'm the same today. I remember once grilling my father endlessly about the construction and operation of a helicopter. I delved deeply into the principles of creating a rotor disk of lift that could be adjusted by the deflection of each blade, and my father helped me to visualize the process, addressing my complex web of questions until my mind was satiated. Understanding how an object moves around has always been much more fun to me than sucking up all the boring rules and methods required to make something operate. When it comes to expanding my mind, I learned from an early age that there is more than one way to skin a cat.

Workshop Notes

HOW TO ASK QUESTIONS
(WITHOUT BEING ANNOYING)

It's a useful fact of life that a lot of people actually love being asked about their work, hobbies or exciting side projects. Most of us like nothing more than to hear the words, 'So, tell me more about that.' It flatters the ego and allows us to express pride in our latest achievements. It's also in those moments that we can vent our frustrations on a failure, or ask for advice on an area in which we may be inexperienced. We can bounce ideas off others.

I was recently at a technology event where I met a guy who was planning to launch the first industrial 3D-printing capability into space. The grand idea was to place a futuristic manufacturing facility within the Earth's orbit in which industrial robots – the 3D printers – received instructions and primary building materials before constructing whatever new satellites or components needed to be put into action. What an amazing thought! In terms of saving costs on rocket launches and construction, it's inspired. Repairs on a malfunctioning weather satellite could be made remotely, in orbit, rather than probably having to be abandoned. There is also the small matter of materials. When building a craft on terra firma it has to be robust enough to withstand the G-forces exerted during take-off and beyond. More reinforcement and protective armour are required to prevent damage as a craft leaves the atmosphere, and by extension, more cash. Constructing something in space would reduce that stress. You could build something fairly brittle and spindly and it would function perfectly well without the forces of gravity testing its metals.

I lapped up the idea, bombarding the pioneer with questions, some of which might have risked sounding somewhat silly or naive to someone of his expertise, but I couldn't help myself. I was intrigued. I've learned that if you frame a series of enquiries in a certain way – basically, with genuine enthusiasm and appreciation – no matter how left-field they might seem to persons of experience or intellect they usually find them engaging. Who doesn't want to be told that what they are passionately investing their time in is fascinating?

For the person answering the questions, these conversations are fun and expressive. And for the inquisitive half of the conversation, this is a moment to learn, an opportunity to pick up a raft of information that may well be helpful later on. I wanted to absorb more science, more intelligence, while collecting a series of unusual theories and plans to store in my brain. Those ideas might resurface someday and connect with another project.

It's not difficult to dig into what a person's passions are and what their background is. Within twenty or thirty minutes it's possible to become semi-expert in what they're about. I think gathering such intelligence is key to innovation: it's about having a disparate playbook of ideas and thoughts, allied to the childlike freedom to say, 'What if I can connect these dots and create something different?'

n 2017, I attended my eldest son's school to deliver a presentation on the jet suit. On a sunny day, I flew around for a brief while and then landed, shutting the engines down to a wall of applause. As I approached the group of children for a quick question-and-answer session, I forgot to switch off the GoPro camera attached to my helmet. It captured every query that was fired at me for the next thirty minutes, which made for some fascinating viewing afterwards.

On the face of it, some of the questions were silly – really silly:

Could you fly to the moon?

Can you fly faster than a fighter plane?

Who's cooler, you or Iron Man?

(Answers: No. No. And, I'd like to think it's me, of course, but my kids are bound to have a different opinion.)

But every now and then a moment of genius was thrown my way. Not, I'd like to point out, because the kid asking the question was necessarily a genius. Instead, they'd followed their free-thinking inclination to question and explore what they had just witnessed such as catching sight of a man in a jet suit flying around a school field for the first time. Think of all the crazy observations, ideas and possibilities that could be triggered in a young mind by such an episode. And so, when one boy asked, 'Could you do back-flips?' I was genuinely inspired. As a result, currently, two gymnastically trained members of my Gravity Industries team are working on that very possibility. Surely, if an acrobat stands rooted to the spot on a solid floor, back-flipping up before returning to the starting position, there is no reason why we can't have a go at the same thing in a jet suit. Through that one boy's innocent strides for knowledge, he had stumbled on a train of thought that was genuinely interesting to a grown man with 35 kilos of jetpack still strapped to his back.

My sons share that same inquisitive nature, twinned with an unabashed desire to ask questions. For the most part their enquiries are fairly amusing, but unrealistic. Every now and then, though, one of them will hit the nail on the head, catching me off guard.

One day, while testing the latest prototype at the farm, I was busy preparing the systems on the tailgate of the Land Rover. I was immersed in the fiddly set-up detail and slightly apprehensive of the ever-present risk of having one of those days when everything goes wrong, you make no progress, and you feed the sceptical voice in your head another few rounds of ammunition. My boys were leaning over the back seats, frankly a bit bored, restless and itching to dash off to play in the woods next to the farmyard. However, for that moment they were actually watching with some interest and started chatting about what they thought would be cool additions to the suit. I have to say I was the stereotypical dismissive parent, pretending to listen, when Oliver came out with it: 'Dad, why couldn't you build an electric jet suit?' The moment is immortalized, as it happens, on an iPhone my wife was recording with. After a few seconds it landed on me, and there was a magic moment when I realized this was actually not a bad idea at all. On the face of it unfeasible and unrealistic, yet that's the business we are in, so we should absolutely not fall at the first hurdle – the pitfall of conventional thinking. We began planning the project the same afternoon.

If Oliver and Thomas are to maintain that inquisitive confidence when confronted with a new idea or experience, I'll have to instil a fair amount of mental fortitude in them. It's very easy to lose heart when our exploratory questions quite plainly frustrate the people around us. It's a process that we teach out of most kids. Instead we push them towards the grades we think they might need to succeed in life, working them into a certain way of thinking in order to tick the boxes required for exam success. If a particular idea can't be found in a textbook, or on the syllabus, then we encourage our next generation of creative thinkers to suppress their wilder thoughts. Sadly, this is often done in such a way that by the time their fertile minds have moved into the adult world they can feel stupid asking the questions that came so naturally to them earlier on in life.

Workshop Notes

THINK LIKE A KID

The older we get, the more reference points we gather and the more our brains become inclined to simplify and make assumptions. We endure a long car journey, see a bridge up ahead, and say, 'Oh, that's a motorway flyover.' Whereas a kid might think, 'Oh look, a motorway skate park! Wouldn't it be cool to rollerskate across *that*?' When it comes to design and creativity, adults are sometimes the enemy of their own thoughts. Childlike thinking is where we let our brains wander, connecting seemingly random ideas rather than dismissing them out of hand as juvenile.

We've been so conditioned by the stresses of modern life that it's often hard to allow ourselves the luxury of thinking like a kid, or daydreaming. We carry an irrepressible inner critic, an internal voice that usually pipes up in a tone befitting a teacher, or parent. When we fantasize, it says, 'Stop mucking about!' It warns us of what might happen were we to fall behind in our studies, or miss our work deadlines. But this expressive way of thinking is so important, whether we're working on a new idea or relaxing at home, because it allows the brain to play, which is an important activity, no matter how old we are, but one we seem to often lose sight of.

Play is where we recuperate and create, forgetting the stresses of the day. And essentially play is at the very heart of the research and development process for every invention. It's the practical way of making something work by physically exploring a concept, by building, by *mucking about*, rather than merely theorizing. When I first worked on the jet suit, many of my breakthrough moments arrived by simply playing around with an idea and some materials, instead of staring at a drawing board and chin-stroking.

I've learned that when the inner critic rises up, that's often the moment we should press ahead with our creativity. We need to enjoy those moments of playfulness, mixing them with a sense of mindfulness in which we become aware that we're expressing ourselves and innovating, rather than simply daydreaming (because the idea of simply daydreaming can make us feel lazy). It's from these moments that the best creative ideas emerge.

There is a wonderful scientific study entitled the Marshmallow Challenge, which highlights the value in childlike thinking and the importance of exploratory recreation. In this experiment, one that has been repeated all over the world, a study group brings together several expert teams, one comprising architects, another military leaders, a group of business leaders and so on. In every session there is also a team of kids, usually around the age of ten. In front of each team, on separate tables, sits some sticky tape, Blu Tack, skewers or spaghetti, elastic bands and one lonely marshmallow. The teams are given a set period of time in which to build a structure that suspends the blob of sugary sickliness as high off the table as possible. For fairness, each group is hidden from the others to ensure that no copying takes place.

What follows is often a hilarious but interesting exercise in which the adults – the supposedly advanced thinkers in the test – spend the majority of the allocated time discussing experience and expertise in order to establish a suitable chain of command. Through that hierarchy they then figure out a way of building the biggest support skyscraper imaginable, but everything is often written down and planned on paper first. Inevitably they are then panicked into action once they've been told that most of their allotted time has been used up in the discussion phase, and in a rush they attempt to see their theories through, only to watch in horror as their construction wobbles and wilts on to the table. (The average marshmallow weighs a lot more than the brain thinks it does. It's a common misconception, one of those weird things in life.) But the kids? They play. They build and fail, then build and fail some more, until eventually a practical technique is stumbled upon and they emerge triumphant with some kind of standing structure, to the surprise of the adults twenty, thirty or forty years their senior.

It's a great and deliberate illustration of the unproductive processes that can occur in big businesses: adults just don't allow themselves that luxury of play, getting their hands on the problem and discovering critical lessons in the process. Theory and debate just don't stand a chance compared to actually picking up the marshmallow. This principle has a significant impact on the pace of innovative change in big business versus smaller and more nimble disruptors.

The lesson here is this: when it comes to expanding the mind, try not to grow up.

Whether we're involved with a new technology, product, or anything creative, simply ask this question: have we surrounded ourselves with existing process, existing status quo thinking, and a disciplined structure? If the answer is 'yes', then our work is only going to move us towards something that has been created already. To be truly innovative, we have to carefully ignore all the rules.

Think about it from a jet suit perspective. Had I told people what I was planning, I'd have been bombarded with votes of no confidence and reminders that I was going against the status quo.

Surely you can't hold a jet engine because the force is unmanageable – you'll never be able to control it.

There might have been criticism.

You're wasting your time. You're being stupid.

But for me, any doubting voices that I did encounter, though often dispiriting, were to my mind good evidence that I was on a path no one had really explored before.

Of course we all have moments when the doubters are proved right. I know. I experienced that as I started my work with Gravity. And yes, I did have to waste my time doing things that were stupid in hindsight, but they were often road signs that said, 'You're at a different place here, playing with stuff that is thought to be pointless, stupid and not worthwhile. In which case you're on prospective hunting ground for new ideas . . .' It was a way of knowing I'd headed in a brave new direction.

Takeaways

○ Question experts with respect, enthusiasm and appreciation. Most people love to be told that what they do is fascinating, and as a result they're often more willing to impart vital knowledge that might become useful later down the line.

○ Embrace the urge to daydream. Rather than dismissing it as a waste of time we should instead allow our minds to wander to unusual places. Play is an essential part of discovery, research and development.

○ Pick up the marshmallow. Ask if your work is surrounded by existing process, dated status quo thinking and stifling structure. If the answer is yes, it's time to introduce some left-field creative thought.

5

JUNIOR ICARUS

Or, Why It Pays Dividends Not to Follow the Crowd

ike most people who consider themselves to be of an adventurous spirit, I was reluctant to follow others as a kid. I've never been one for moving with a crowd. I didn't support a football team at school and I've never been part of a music tribe. (My very first cassette was Michael Jackson's *Bad*, which came out in 1987.) Meanwhile, as various crazes passed through my school – *Star Wars* collectibles, yo-yos, breakdancing, BMX riding – I mostly remained a content observer, far more interested to play at the edges of whatever scene or social grouping was in vogue at the time. From there I delighted in doing my own thing with a few close friends, all the while keeping an eye on what was going on within the majority. I was very much an individual, and even today I'm useless at small talk. I'm rubbish at hanging out in a collective, shooting the breeze with others. Weirdly, I don't see the point. I've also never been one to fetishize other individuals, or their achievements. I have minimal interest in watching other people doing cool stuff, but I'm always up for getting involved. For example, I've been to a couple of F1 Grand Prix events and found the spectator experience to be really quite boring after the initial impact wears off. But if somebody were to offer me a shot at burning around the track in a high-powered McLaren, I'd jump at the chance.

As a kid, I didn't become a loner. I was pleasant, sociable. In a way, I wasn't unlike one of those penguins you might see on a nature documentary – a large group of them huddling together for warmth for days on end as a vicious snowstorm rages around them. Only I was constantly at the edges of the group, close enough to stay warm but not so close to the middle that I was completely ensconced and unable to do my own thing. To extend the analogy, I couldn't have entirely distanced myself from the school groups playing with their *Star Wars* toys or riding their BMXs because I'd have frozen to death – socially, at least. Only those individuals with the necessary survival skills and supreme confidence to go it alone can operate successfully as total loners in the playground, or the Arctic wilderness.

It's what set me on a path to become the person I am today.

I was the same when I later worked as an oil trader, a position I held in the latter half of my sixteen-year career with BP in London. Generous bonuses, not quite of the kind made famous by newspaper headlines in recent years, were typically paid out once a year, and in the days immediately afterwards, it wasn't uncommon for traders flush with cash to splurge their earnings on decadent rewards. We'd all hear tales of huge bills run up in champagne bars, and blokes turning up in the office sporting outrageously expensive watches or boasting about their new cars, alerting everybody working within their vicinity to the extent of their spending power. My direct experience wasn't quite as extreme as those stereotypes, but the underlying culture was certainly there and I could never quite get my head around it.

A funny thing always happened within a week of those extravagant spending sprees: the shine wore off. The glow created by the brain's risk and reward mechanism diminished; the dopamine hit faded from the system. Traders now found themselves shackled to the realities of their new toys. The shiny new penthouse flat demanded a bigger mortgage repayment. Meanwhile, insurance didn't come cheap for the new yacht owners, while the cost of mooring somewhere nice was sometimes incredibly pricey. Workers who had momentarily been adrenalized by the success of their annual efforts were suddenly chained to the next year's bonus. The pressure was on to repeat and beat their big score, and they became slaves to their own ego. A lot of people had to make more money, and generate more returns, if they were to keep up with the repayments on their last lot of spoils, and they were stuck on a hamster wheel that was very difficult to jump off.

Without getting snooty about it, the City's spend, spend, spend mentality wasn't something I ever subscribed to. I continued to do my own thing on the peripheries of the trading floor as I developed my career and received bonuses of my own. I had zero interest in the keeping-up-with-the-Joneses mind-set. It seemed uninspiring, so I rebelled against it. Rather than buy a fancy, overpriced watch as a statement to prove to people just how much money I'd made, I opted for a cheapo number from Amazon that I could wear in the swimming pool or the gym. That was my quiet snub to the culture going on around me of spending for spending's sake.

In work, and before then when I was growing up, I always observed the games that people played without becoming so immersed in them that I couldn't spot new patterns or new emerging ideas elsewhere. When I was younger, some of those off-kilter and away-from-the-mainstream activities took place with my dad, and I was forever learning in his workshop, probably while my mates were out playing football. This gave me an invaluable perspective on life and creativity and from an early age I was able to spot the wood from the trees.

Let me give you a little backstory to explain.

Life as a jet suit test pilot began when I was young, very young, an only kid living with my parents in Camberley, the leafy enclave in Surrey where Dad – Michael Browning – worked for a nearby aeronautics company. He was a maverick creator, an aeronautical engineer by profession, and I grew up messing around in his homespun workshop as he loomed over a bench where bits of aluminium were always being machined or assembled with an endless array of nuts, bolts and fixings. Despite the slightly hazardous surroundings, and the fact that I'd only just learned to read and write, I was entrusted from a young age and rarely restricted in what I could and couldn't play around with. One of my favourite times of the year was always the weeks leading up to Fireworks Night, when we'd buy as many rockets and Catherine wheels as we could justify, strip away the flashy, colourful outer wrapping and liberate the explosive materials packed inside. It was always slightly risky work, but Dad kept an eye on me throughout and allowed me to build my confidence and manage the process. I still possess every major limb and appendage so I guess it worked.

Our endgame in this potentially hazardous *Blue Peter*-style project was to build a three-stage rocket, which comprised a trio of different-sized tubes packed with a core of propellant and slotted on top of one another, connected by the wooden stick found in most cheap rockets. Our grand displays, when they eventually took place on 5 November, always began with me lighting the bottom 'fuel tank', which propelled our construction moonward as the burning materials inside eventually caught the tail-end of the smaller, second rocket above. In a style not too dissimilar to an early NASA space launch, the empty lower carcass fell away, then the middle one, and then the lead tube exploded up to a seriously impressive altitude. These were modest attempts at reaching a Brave New World, but to my mind I was playing on the edge of danger and achieving something very cool.

Most pioneers meet an influential character during their formative years. There are so many narratives where a famous somebody has the course of their journey altered for ever by someone close to them: the record-breaking sports star and his or her grizzled coach, or the rock singer and their older sibling, handed down a life-altering album that changes their creative worldview dramatically, inspiring them to make something special of their own life. Mum was key to a lot of things in my life, especially once my father had passed away, but Dad played a pivotal role in what would become a career in jet suit construction from day one, mainly through his enthusiasm for science and engineering, but more importantly with his love of *playing* with ideas and theories. From an early age his mind-set was transposed on to me, and as soon as I was old enough we'd build mini model aeroplanes as a dynamic duo, the constructions pieced together with balsa wood and glue, stretched and 'doped' tissue paper cladding the structure, before they were launched across the expanse of our modest lawn, often for hours on end.

Eventually this obsession with engines and speed took us into some pretty exciting areas. Well, exciting to a small boy at least, especially one obsessed with danger, bangs and explosions. I remember putting together a Lego boat that chugged along the local pond for a brief moment, propelled by the same firework material used for launching our homemade rockets. Inevitably, the rocket motor was never going to be set at the optimum angle to transfer the burst of thrust through the boat's centre of mass. Unfazed, Dad lit the fuse and the rocket whooshed into life, although hilariously it immediately ploughed the boat underwater and drove it with some aggression along the bottom of the shallow pond. But I wasn't bothered by the loss. The sense of adventure in building the vessel had been overwhelming. Meanwhile, the element of (slight) danger and potential disappointment in everything Dad and I did together in those days felt insignificant when our projects did come together. Messing about with him was so thrilling.

I loved getting my hands dirty, either through the process of building something from scratch, or tearing it apart. Every time we lost a household appliance to age or disrepair I'd relish the opportunity to break down its carcass, the electrical innards spilling across the floor as Dad looked on proudly. One time I even pulled apart an old cathode ray TV set, which maybe wasn't a great idea in hindsight. Once it had been rendered inoperable, I unplugged the thing and laid down a dustsheet in the living room, all the while being encouraged to explore its insides.

'All yours, Richard,' Dad said enthusiastically, before leaving the room, unaware of what was to happen.

I prised away the outer case and loosened the screws, immediately becoming fascinated by what looked like a cityscape of wires and components. In the heart of it all was a delicate lightbulb-like feature, a fitting I later learned was the cathode ray tube, which contained the electron gun to fire a picture at the back of the phosphorescent screen. I gingerly tapped it with a hammer, but nothing happened.

'Hmm,' I thought. 'Maybe I should hit it a bit harder.'

When I then delivered a sharp blow to the structure, it splintered dramatically with an implosive bang. It was like a small improvised explosive device had gone off in the otherwise peaceful environs of our suburban home. I experienced a flash of panic. For a fraction of a second my eyes felt like they were being pulled from their sockets. The vacuum in the TV tube was so powerful and perfectly contained that it had generated a massive gulp of suction, fortunately pulling the shards of glass inwards as well. If we'd had Google in those days, it's highly unlikely Dad would have let me anywhere near such a potentially explosive piece of equipment with a screwdriver and a hammer.

Together we bonded over our love of aircraft and cars. I became intrigued by man's advancements in the fields of flight and speed and where things might go in the future. If any new engineering development was loud, fast or airborne we usually became very enthusiastic about it. But most of all we loved creating together, taking an idea or blueprint and building whatever it was to a point where we could test it in the garden, or in the countryside.

Of these adventures, the one that most sticks in my mind is our project to build a remote-controlled model glider, which involved the same pain-in-the-arse construction process as our balsa-wood planes, but with a two-channel radio-controlled flight system in place. Technically it wouldn't have been too dissimilar to the control mechanism that could be found in any basic remote-controlled car set: our system had the same forwards, backwards, left and right functions, but instead of moving the wheels, our remote guided the elevators and rudder of a simple glider, which we then flew from the grassy slopes of Corton Hill in Dorset, watching as our homemade bird sat in the updraught for what seemed like hours. Those adventures with Dad were like magic to me.

Without knowing it, my brain was being hooked on to the principles and visual dynamics of flight.

I liked the idea of one day owning a loud and fast car. On my wall there was a poster of a Ferrari 308 GT4, which I thought looked

81

spectacular, though I wasn't opposed to bombing around in our little Mini. Mum and Dad used to have a yellow one on the driveway, and given its modest size it seemed very accessible: I reasoned I didn't need to be that big to drive it around town, and I daydreamed about doing up its engine and exterior into something much more fun-looking. I also became interested in pioneering spirits such as the Virgin entrepreneur Sir Richard Branson, who by that time had made several attempts to travel across oceans and around the globe in a variety of different craft with varying degrees of success, most notably his hot-air balloon, the *Virgin Atlantic Flyer*, in 1987. To my thinking, Branson was a very successful but normal business guy doing something crazy and pioneering, and somehow not being overly chastised for taking a risk and often failing. I seemed to connect with his sense of adventure.

Weirdly, though, my interest didn't extend to interplanetary travel or NASA's all-powerful space programme, which was forever launching high-profile shuttles and satellites into the skies. To dream of being an astronaut felt distant to me because the fantasy was almost too obvious. Every boy in the world wanted to fly into space, and NASA was only ever going to pick one or two highly trained near-superhumans for the gig. So with the odds already stacked against my commanding an exploratory craft, I don't think the idea ever really took root for me. I was a strangely pragmatic child in that way, socially a modest introvert but also full of self-belief: I'd decided that if I was to boldly go somewhere new, or scary, I wanted to do it travelling by an unusual, pioneering method, something that had never been done before. To take the unconventional route seemed so much more exciting.

As a kid, flight never left my way of thinking, which was unsurprising, given that it was very much in the family gene pool. My grandfather on Dad's side was a career airline pilot for BEA and a number of other companies that acted as precursors to British Airways after World War Two. Most impressively, he also instructed for the RAF and taught on a number of fighter and light bomber aircraft, such as the Blenheim, as well as conducting a large number of operational tours. On my mum's side, my other grandfather was Sir Basil Blackwell, who ran the Westland helicopter company during the 1970s and 1980s. Westland was famous for building the Lynx, Sea King and Merlin helicopters, and one of the upsides of being related to Sir Basil was that I was often taken aboard the company's creations, though I was too young to remember the flights. Granddad had an amazing life even before he embarked on his business career. He emerged from a fairly tough childhood under his domineering mother in Leeds to qualify, on merit, for a place at Cambridge University, where he claimed a double first in Maths and Classics. Once World War Two had broken out, his education meant he was placed within the world of naval intelligence, where he helped to locate and destroy Germany's fearsome fleet of U-boats. In later life he was knighted for his services to the aerospace industry.

Given this creative, pioneering and slightly eccentric backdrop, is it any wonder I eventually strapped jet engines to my body and fired myself towards the clouds?

Being happy in my own company was something I excelled at as I grew up, though it wasn't as if I didn't have any friends. Instead I realized that I was more than content when messing around by myself at home, or in the woods that backed on to our garden. During holidays and weekends, away from schoolmates and without a brother or sister to play with, I discovered I had more than enough imagination to keep me occupied. It also helped that I had a wild playground to explore just seconds from my back door. The family home in Camberley, which was located on the Blackwater housing estate, was built alongside Hawley Lake, an area used by the military to train soldiers, including officer recruits working from the Royal Military Academy at Sandhurst. Also Aldershot, the town from which the

Parachute Regiment worked, was near by and noisy war games often took place a mile or two behind the garden. When the shouting and explosive banging calmed down I was able to open my back gate and step into a world of military-inspired fantasy.

Sometimes I was accompanied by friends from junior school, but often I was alone, and I'd walk for hours on end, exploring man-made tunnels and trenches while hiding from passers-by as I pretended to be engaged in a covert Army mission against an imagined force of baddies. My parents expected me to be sensible, and God knows how, but I seemed to have built up their trust from around the age of seven or eight, though my mum would often have palpitations if ever I stayed out beyond the agreed curfew time. The Broadmoor Mental Health Hospital was also near by and occasionally they tested their sirens (or maybe used them for real), which I guess was to alert the locals to the possibility of an escaped patient. If ever the alarms sounded and I was out in the woods alone, Mum would have a minor meltdown.

Those woods were quiet, idyllic, with plenty of hidey-holes to escape into – a boys' paradise. And because the area had been a military training zone for over fifty years there were all kinds of treasures to be found. In some places the tracks of Army vehicles had churned up the ground into muddy pathways, and there was an old wartime runway to play upon. At bedtime I would listen out for all the tell-tale signs of a night operation – the shouts of soldiers issuing fire control orders during a mock ambush, the cracks of blank rounds and flash bang grenades in the distance – and from under my covers I'd attempt to pinpoint the roar of machine-gun fire to some sector of the woods, knowing I would visit there as soon as it was safe to venture beyond the garden gate the next morning. I had a magpie instinct for where the action had taken place and would retrace a criss-cross of muddy footprints like a forensic scientist, seeking out any detritus or souvenirs that might have been left behind. Though it wasn't allowed, taking home a spent round was considered a jackpot.

I didn't need *Battle* or *Eagle* comics or a book full of football stickers because I was surrounded by real-life action, the kind most people only saw at the pictures. One day, as I hid behind the bushes near one of the Army's crudely constructed landing zones, three Chinook helicopters swooped from the skies and a unit of soldiers leapt out, running away from the rotor blades' down force and into the vegetation, where their shouting and gunfire echoed around the woods. They were extracted by the same choppers minutes later. Every incident, every moment of adventure, fuelled my unbounded sense of freedom. I didn't live in a high-rise flat, I wasn't overly constrained by my parents or a fear of what was happening in the Real World; I was lucky enough to be surrounded by nature, and a pretend war was frequently playing out minutes away from my bedroom window. Why would I need a box of plastic toys or mind-numbing video games to feed my fantasies?

Bullets and bunkers weren't the only outlets for my febrile imagination. In my bedroom, on a worktop affixed across the top of a pine chest of drawers, I could often be found chiselling away at the latest fossil I'd uncovered in the mud somewhere. Usually they would be collected from Sherborne in Dorset, where my maternal grandparents lived, and I'd get a real kick whenever I saw something dark and shiny protruding from the sandstone as we went on walks together. More often than not it would be nothing more than a rock, but there were one or two occasions when I was lucky enough to find a dark ammonite, and with my angle-lamp poised above my 'workbench' at home I would spend hours chipping away at the edges of the long-extinct marine mollusc, pretending to be a palaeontologist at the site of the remains of some previously unseen prehistoric beast, losing myself in the detail and wonderment of a once-living thing. Like those dismantled household appliances and our exploding telly, I loved exploring the intricacy of an object, whether it was natural or man-made.

My sense of adventure was heightened even further when Dad decided to buy me an air rifle. I was probably only eight years old, and I'd imagine that today a purchase of that kind for such a young lad would be frowned upon. But my parents subscribed to a trust-based code of familial care. In their heads they were exposing me to carefully managed danger, such as being allowed to roam the woods alone, and though playing around with a gun of that kind was vaguely hazardous, the odds of serious injury were low. Their thinking was that my exposure to a measure of jeopardy meant that I'd learn to take responsibility and be even more careful when firing the thing. It is a theory I have since tried to pass on to my own kids. I'm usually happy for them to smelt aluminium or build homemade fireworks under strict supervision, knowing that the perceived risk of causing harm to themselves encourages an attitude of self-care and responsibility.

Both my sons light up if ever I show them something new that we might be able to drive, fly, shoot or blow up together. I have an incredible photo of the look on Oliver's face when we once melted down some aluminium and copper offcuts in a makeshift furnace made from a stack of old breeze blocks, an electric lilo pump blowing air down a rusty metal tube and into the base of a charcoal fire. With our safety specs on (of course) we poured the molten metal into a homemade sand cast, which was supposed to depict a crudely constructed Lego man. It was creative, dangerous, visceral, and he probably shouldn't have been doing it, but it was his idea of heaven. I'd like to think that Oliver and Thomas learn a lot on days like that one. It's when people *aren't* familiar with risk that they tend to hurt themselves. Cocooned by a perpetual safety blanket, they can become careless and blind to potential dangers.

Ironically, with hindsight, the fact that my air rifle was so low-powered actually made it more hazardous to use. I would aim it at a plywood target board set up in the garden, but sometimes when I pulled the trigger a high-pitched whizzing sound trailed the projectile. Rather than sticking into it with a satisfying thud, the pellet would ricochet off the wood and, with a sharp jab, into my chest – there simply wasn't enough velocity for it to pierce its intended target.

Graduating to a better air rifle in my early teens, I'd often take it on my travels in the woods, where I'd make a camouflaged foxhole for myself. The game was to wait patiently, hoping for an unsuspecting rabbit or pigeon to cross my path; I could then take it down with my low-powered hunting machine. Luckily for them, and despite fairly proficient powers of concealment, the range of this newer rifle was still miserable. Happily my success rate remained disappointingly low, but the buzz of it all was enough to keep me going back for ages.

Workshop Notes

BE THE PENGUIN ON THE OUTSIDE

Within a raft of industries the idea of operating on the periphery is somewhat suited to working on a new idea, one that nobody has thought of before. It allows a person to remain connected to incumbent knowledge and expertise, but at the same time to remain liberated enough to question and challenge such influences. Be the penguin on the outside: do just enough to stay warm, but don't move so deep into the colony that you can't pick up on new ideas from elsewhere.

Working as an individual can pay dividends. I've found it's much better to be within touching distance of a working community rather than being ensconced in it. It's good to recognize when being sucked along by trends at work. Sure, notice what's going on, lurk around the edges; appear to play in the same area, but stay slightly removed.

This allows us to spot the interesting patterns elsewhere while carving out some fairly unique working practices for ourselves. (You'll find out exactly how I did that in chapter 8.)

It's not easy, however.

I imagine that if we bumped into James Dyson as he began his journey into reimagining the vacuum cleaner from the peripheries of a busy industry, a market dominated by the likes of Hoover and Electrolux, there might have been some doubt over the validity of his work. After all, a number of electrical manufacturers were already cleaning up in that corner of the market, figuratively and literally. Yet Dyson pressed on regardless. He avoided sliding towards existing solutions; he ignored the collective thought that figured his cyclonic vacuum cleaner would fall by the wayside. Today the results speak for themselves. Dyson constructed a product that reimagined the concept of a vacuum cleaner and on its introduction his Dual Cyclone became the quickest-selling product on the market.

Takeaways

○ We should expose ourselves to a little danger when being creative, and learn to manage risk. Risk is a key part of innovation and discovery, and when people become insulated or sheltered from it they are unprepared when real threats present themselves.

○ Don't follow the herd. Avoid being a slave to trends. Instead, be like the outsider penguin and operate on the peripheries, where you can observe what's happening away from the crowd.

○ Always be careful when dismantling a cathode ray TV set!

THE EXPLORER GENE

Or, How Genetics Schools Us for a
Lifetime of Creativity

xactly what was the childlike urge that compelled me to fly? Or, more specifically, what was it that inspired a perfectly rational bloke to attach a series of micro gas turbines to his body and bearing 144 kilos of thrust before powering himself into the air? The risks, which would have presented massive psychological hurdles to most people, are simply too terrifying to ignore, and for good reason too. The possible hazards included: serious injury, especially were I to push the suit to its full capacity of many hundreds of mph; potential financial ruin, should my business plans go badly wrong; and a very public humiliation, if either of these hazards were to take place. And yet I happily worked in the face of those threats because the rewards were worth it, not least the adrenalized, gratifying and exciting surge to the brain that inspired me to lift off again and again. *And then again.* Moreover, my desire to fly and to explore was in all likelihood rooted in the same genetic coding that's been located in approximately 20 per cent of the planet's population – the 1.5 billion of us looking to pioneer a wild new idea, some strange hunch or untested theory, innovation hardwired into our brains through the lottery of DNA.

The science behind this statement is fairly well known, and was written about in *National Geographic* magazine in 2013. For one fifth of the globe's inhabitants, the need to explore hostile jungles or aim satellites for the stars and planets beyond our solar system is tied up with the DRD4 gene, which manages the release of dopamine into the body's central nervous system. For those readers not overly familiar with neuroscience, dopamine is produced by the brain's reward-motivating mechanisms and it delivers a sense of excitement, or wellbeing, whenever we achieve our targets. *It drives us.* Scoring the winning goal in a World Cup final, landing a lucrative business contract, or running a 5K race for the first time all bring lovely hits of dopamine. All of us are loaded with the DRD4 gene, but it's an accompanying strand, known as DRD4-7R, that's been linked to risk-taking, exploration and inquisitiveness, and it's present in 20 per cent of the human race, give or take. It can't be created artificially; those people who possess DRD4-7R are born with it. The astronaut Neil Armstrong, the inventor Elon Musk and the explorer Christopher Columbus were probably powered by the stuff as they embarked upon their pioneering adventures. Maybe I'm in the afflicted 20 per cent too.

The theory is that this particular gene strand might have played a major role in our species' evolution over time. The idea is impossible to prove, given we don't have a time machine to conduct any DNA tests on cavemen, but it suggests that *Homo sapiens'* production of DRD4-7R-leaning individuals in the early Neanderthal years could have had plenty to do with our survival, especially in the midst of a harsh battle of the fittest where we strived to live alongside sabre-toothed tigers and stampeding mammoths. Today the gene strand is attributed to people who regularly experience a sense of wander-lust. Among the early tribes beginning our migration across the face of the Earth all those tens of thousands of years ago, the most likely groups to succeed were those who followed a leader with an inquisi-tive mind. Perhaps DRD4-7R played its part.

It's an interesting thought. Let's say there were two tribes, side by side, both living in similar environments. Which one was most likely to win out: the collective that stayed rooted in the same space, fearing the wrath of some angry sun god should they abandon a hand-carved totem of his likeness for pastures new; or the group that aban-doned their home to explore further afield, seeking out a better source of water, or a greater supply of food? Because if a tribe didn't have a sprinkling of curious individuals within their group – the caveman trying to fashion a new sword; the cavewoman building an exploratory water well – and if there wasn't a tolerance for inquisitive behaviour within their numbers, that collective would remain stranded, unable to progress or evolve. They would most probably die out after a time. The human race has always needed great thinkers in order to progress.

By mapping genetic footprints across the globe, scientists have theorized that early man first ventured from his birthplace in Africa some 60,000 or 70,000 years ago. The reason for this first migration was the weather. *It was bloody cold.* Studies have pointed to the fact that the Ice Age cooled the continent significantly at that time, reducing the world's human population to around 10,000. As people dropped dead with hypothermia and starvation, the survivor's instinct kicked in. Somebody must have suggested the idea of moving elsewhere to prevent extinction. The Eurasian regions were explored first by some travellers. Evidence suggests that other groups later headed towards the Middle East and into southern Central Asia several thousand years later. This journey has continued throughout history. Today, very little of the planet remains untouched by our footprints.

The need to roam is one thing, but what caused our fascination with the skies above us? From the very first Chinese kite flights, which were invented thousands of years ago, to the first parachute drop completed by André-Jacques Garnerin in 1797, and, most recently, the first solar-powered journey around the world in 2016, humankind has been completely and utterly obsessed with the idea of getting our heads into the clouds, in a literal sense. I'd imagine it probably started with those early tribes. As they left the sanctuaries of their dank and gloomy caves they must have watched in awe as birds circled overhead before proclaiming, 'Wow, that's cool . . . but how do *we* get up there?'

This audacious spirit has never left us. The exploration of flight is a perfect indicator of our desire to go above and beyond, to think big and push boundaries, and it has attracted the biggest dreamers and innovators, such as Leonardo da Vinci, who in the late fifteenth century, alongside his incredible paintings and artistic studies of human anatomy, spent a vast amount of time designing flying machines such as the helicopter – which he imagined to be man-powered, with physical labour working the rotary blades – and making sketches for parachutes. Why did he return to the concept of flight so often? Because the sky was an obvious realm in which humans didn't naturally exist, and yet it was around us, all the time. We marvelled at it – a lot of us still do.

As with early man, when the decision was taken to step away from their homes in order to survive, bravery has always been at the heart of flight exploration. Imagine the heart rates of Jean-François Pilâtre de Rozier and the Marquis d'Arlandes as they drifted up into the air to make the first aerial voyage in a hot-air balloon designed by the Montgolfier brothers in 1783. The experience must have been terrifying. De Rozier lost his life a couple of years later while attempting to cross the English Channel in a balloon, and sadly the history of exploration is littered with the bodies of inventors whose ideas failed spectacularly. It's a sobering lesson for all of us. But I believe that while the jet suit operates in the same arena, I hardly share the same risks as experienced, for instance, by test pilots commanding the German-built Heinkel 178 – the first fully jet-propelled plane to fly, in 1939.

Today, advancements in jet engine technology are so impressive that the concept is almost dismissed as being another part of modern life, like TV remote controls and Wi-Fi. We only have to peer upwards to glimpse the outline of a Boeing 747 as it glides between the clouds, 300 tonnes of aluminium and jet fuel seemingly moving effortlessly as the few hundred passengers relaxing quietly inside eat their lunch and watch a selection of Hollywood films on the in-flight entertainment system. Had such a vision been mooted to people three hundred years ago, the idea would have been dismissed as witchcraft, yet here we are in the twenty-first century with tens of thousands of passengers in the air at any one time – and statistically safer up there than a pedestrian walking across a busy city street.

Our relationship with flight has proved to me that as a species we can be very resourceful when we want to achieve something. When it comes to extracting energy reserves we're able to position an oil rig such that it can lower a drill column through several thousand feet of water, and then into a stretch of varying rock formations to hit a target the size of a basketball deep in the Earth's crust. If we suddenly discovered a rare Earth element that was abundant on Pluto, something that might provide a free, limitless and environmentally friendly energy source, we'd probably be there within a couple of years. Like the soldier making his way out of the jungle with two broken legs, or Aron Ralston, the climber who in 2003 famously became trapped by a rock and was forced to cut off his own arm with a blunt knife to free himself, *we'd find a way.*

The human instinct for survival is endlessly fascinating and that same desire, twinned with the DRD4-7R gene, has driven us as a species to achieve in every direction and in every realm, from science and sport to art and architecture. But the ultimate ambition remains: the defiance of that perpetual master, gravity; to be as free as a bird in the sky without the encumbrance of stepping into a plane, helicopter or hot-air balloon, moving at faster speeds and greater altitudes. As a species we hate denial; we dislike obstacles to progression. We despise being told, 'No.' Thankfully, when it comes to propelling ourselves up, up and away it's a word we've been disregarding for nearly 250 years. We've put gravity on notice and said, 'We're doing this!'

I suppose much of this ambition is the result of circumstance. Had we been born with tentacles rather than legs the very act of walking freely, or running, would have seemed superhuman. Designing something that unlocked our bonds, allowing us to sprint around like a pack of slower, less charismatic Usain Bolts, would have been both mind-bending and liberating. To my thinking, gravity is still our ball and chain, man-made flight our thrilling escape from it; a suit that allows us to fly across the horizon like a Marvel Comics superhero has to some become the ultimate expression of freedom. For most of us, the sensation of flying around with the birds is limited to feel-good dreams that usually happen when we're psychologically at a healthy point in our lives. In the real world things might be going swimmingly and then, in our snoring state, we lift from the ground in a swell of euphoria, rise into the blue and arc over buildings like a real-life Superman, or Supergirl.

To me, that psychological experience has become the mother-of-all-metaphors. Awake, we're restricted, shackled to Earth by gravity. Asleep, we're free, our subconscious making a mockery of the impossible.

D ad carried the explorer gene for sure, but he also had a rough time with his work and often struggled financially while attempting to commercialize his entrepreneurial breakthroughs. I have vague recollections of him packing in the security of his job with an aeronautics company to follow his dreams of becoming an inventor – and back then he had plenty of ideas about where his work might take him. Dad had designed a small-wheeled racing bike that was even more aerodynamic than a normal bike. He'd also made plans for an interesting folding bicycle, not dissimilar to the type you see everywhere in big cities today but vastly more compact. But he believed the brand Moulton had cornered what was considered a niche market back then and his biggest hopes became tied to a new design for what he thought would be a revolutionary mountain bike suspension system.

In the early years of mountain bike evolution, a few mountain bikes had a pair of suspension units fitted within the fork, but Dad had another idea: what would happen if you could suspend that fork within the headset of the bike itself? Any initial obstacles to that design – the reality that the suspension system would rotate as you moved, incapacitating the steering – were soon overcome by a steering link, the kind that can be found on the nose landing gear of an

97

aircraft. With his home-crafted blueprints in place, Dad soon felt constrained by his day job, like any inventive force would, especially one with a revolutionary idea. I think most entrepreneurs, tied to their desk in a nine-to-five role, feel a loss of freedom. The brain doesn't have the space to explore and becomes bored; any desire to try new ideas is held back by orthodoxy. And all the while there is a tendency to wonder, 'I could do what we make here so much better myself . . .' Sometimes those hunches are proved right and a person is set free in a blaze of glory. At other times, the harsh realities of working alone, exposed, can hit a person very hard.

And it would come to hit Dad very hard.

To give you an idea of what my father was like at that time, I've got a story that perfectly sums up his individualism. I remember we were all at a family gathering. I was fairly young and it had been a tedious occasion for all of us. There was probably a lot of small talk to get through. I've grown up with a similar personality to my dad so I can now fully appreciate his aversion to endless polite conversation. But then Dad did what most people wish they could do when faced with the prospect of sitting right the way through a gruelling social event: he quietly left the room, retiring to the solitude of our car to get on with some design work in his notebook while the party played out. I don't think it was viewed as a rude gesture. *It's just Michael doing what he does.* And there was no suggestion he didn't like any of the other guests – he did, dearly. It was just that in that moment Dad had coldly assessed the situation and decided he wasn't enjoying himself. The boredom had become too much for him, and rather than endure it wearing a false rictus grin he'd walked away instead. These days I look at that as being quite a brave move. Who hasn't wished they could act in a similar way when stuck at a dull party?

Dad was also a dreamer. He was able to get very excited about an idea and where a person could go with it, like any innovative or creative mind is able to do. I remember him once suggesting a plan to build a light aircraft of his own and I was amazed at the very idea a person could do that alone. But then my father was surprising in so many ways. He made the impossible seem possible, and his energy and passion were infectious; from an engineering point of view I don't think he believed there were many challenges that were beyond him. I often got the sense from Dad that adventures were there to be cherished, none more so than when he told me about the time he'd once hitchhiked across North Africa, thinking it would be a fun thing to do – which it was, apparently.

Sadly, there was a flipside to his ambition and spirit of derring-do. I wasn't entirely sure of the concept of someone being bipolar when I was a kid – like a lot of people back then, I probably put it down to bad moods, or grumpiness – but I definitely noticed that for all his visionary thinking and optimistic fantasizing, there were occasionally dark moments. Nothing was ever diagnosed, but I think Dad experienced disproportionate emotional highs and lows to the people moving within his orbit. This is something I have come to recognize in myself at times: I've allowed myself to get carried away with the possibilities and potential of an idea to the point of being exuberant and then, when it's not worked out as well as I'd hoped, I've wallowed in a bout of self-doubt and regret. *Why did you do that? How ridiculous to imagine it might work. You idiot!* When a brain is set that way, in addition to a psychological condition, a person can experience quite a kaleidoscope of emotional colours.

Once my father had decided to strike out on his own, I did pick up on an increasing level of stress within the family home, as any small boy would. Mum's senior but very stressful job in senior management at a high-end City insurance firm meant she was having to work really hard, and her pay packets were bankrolling the loans taken out to finance Dad's business. They'd also remortgaged the house. As I got older, I became painfully aware of how his successful breakthroughs simply weren't turning into profitable successes and that certain people – potential investors and partners – were letting him down by not coming through with promised money or support, which must have been heart-breaking. I was receiving first hand a practical, worst-case-scenario lesson of how damn hard it is to run a business. But I know his lack of success wasn't the result of a half-hearted attitude, or a lack of determination. I was always aware of my father's slightly left-field attitudes towards moving forward on a project and he would take bold measures, risks even, to enhance its chances of success.

I can distinctly remember him buying several doves from Richard Branson's parents. I think he'd heard they were breeders of some kind and Dad must have got it into his head that by making friends with the family there was a small chance he would link up with the master-mind behind the Virgin Group. Maybe together they would forge a creative alliance that would see them scale my dad's business. Well, that was the theory anyway. At the time we lived on a housing estate in Camberley in a nice four-bedroom house, but the garden was rather small, which made it a somewhat awkward location for a dovecote. Then, having met with the Branson family's senior members, it became clear that any access to Richard was unlikely. Given that this was the only reason for meeting them in the first place, Dad now found we were lumbered with three doves – three doves that attracted a horde of amorous pigeons, which left grim splatters of bird poop wherever they landed. At times our patio was so messy it looked like a plasterer's radio.

Looking back, I think Dad was somewhat ahead of the curve in business terms. These days, the very culture of start-ups and their position within modern, conventional industry is part of the main-stream narrative: everybody seems to know somebody who is either leading one themselves or has an interest in one. Self-employed and freelance figures are very much a benchmark of entrepreneurship in modern society. But back then, Dad was forever having to field awk-ward questions from friends and family. *Why did you give up a perfectly good day job? What are you going to do for a pension?* And when he later accepted investment from his side of the family, the pressure on him only intensified.

One thing I've learned from my father's experience is that I would prefer to avoid financial help from family and friends. It's an unnecessary extra layer of stress. Any investment in an idea should be based on its potential for success; it shouldn't be a goodwill or sympathy gesture from a friend. Accepting money on that basis flouts the sort of sensible due diligence any investment opportunity requires; and once a person has taken that route, their personal relationships are placed under tension. Dad was under serious stress, even though everyone who saw his mountain bike suspension regarded it as being superbly innovative. But as I've since learned, having a good idea is only one small part of the job. Finding a route to market, with the right branding and the right manufacturing and commercial support structure, is where the real business is done. Dad was working in a competitive, self-funded environment that was much less supportive than it would be today. His progress was happening too slowly. Development costs spiralled. He was soon struggling under the burden.

Weirdly, even at a young age I had a keen sense for the importance of earning money, as some kids are naturally inclined to do. I felt a desire to be financially secure; in order to earn the biggest pay cheques I wanted to know what career I should work towards. I wasn't greedy, I simply needed to see a stable future somewhere in the middle distance. Not all kids are like that, I know. Most of them seem quite happy to dance into the next adventure while not giving a crap, but even then I was squirrelling away cash, *pennies*, into a savings account like a junior Sir Alan Sugar. I was financially practical and most people would probably have regarded me as a very serious kid. Despite my propensity to get excited by an innovative idea or the potential of an engineering development, I wasn't one for completely living in a fantasy land.

This trait was only heightened by my father's business problems, and late one evening I heard my parents in the kitchen. I knew the argument was largely about money, and sensing their precarious position I crept downstairs in my pyjamas.

'Hey Dad, I've got a couple of hundred pounds in my savings account,' I said. 'I'm happy to give it to you if it helps.'

The gesture was entirely well meaning, but it must have been a tragic moment for them both, my innocent offering of aid only exacerbating the sense that the Browning family was in a fairly messy spot.

Their suffering at that time would mark me for years to come.

Workshop Notes

FIND YOUR RECOVERABILITY
FACTOR IN TIMES OF STRESS

Dad had placed all his eggs into one basket. He'd manoeuvred himself into a position where his energy and resources were focused on one idea, one plan, and if it went horribly wrong then everything would crash down around him. His work became an all-or-nothing gamble where the pressure was overwhelming, and his evenings must have been an endless series of unpleasant questions and flashes of self-doubt.

If this doesn't work, what am I going to do with my life?

Who am I going to let down?

How am I going to live with myself?

Through watching Dad's struggles, I understood the importance of having more than one project on the go at any given time, because pursuing an innovative idea or one single development direction is high-risk – the odds are stacked against success. Learning that fact is key.

Think of the work as a multi-round boxing match: if one punch winds us and we're on the floor in a flood of tears, then it's unlikely we'll succeed as innovators. Like a boxer, we have to protect ourselves. In this line of work, having an outlet, or outlets, through which to recover from disappointment becomes vital. It means that whenever we're having a down moment, whenever we suffer a setback, it's possible to focus on and draw strength from other important areas in our lives.

To build that shield, I've often taken a portfolio attitude to the entrepreneurial journey. Consider life as a *series* of projects: work, sport or hobbies, home life, entrepreneurial ideas, and so on. Of the five or six things I've often had going on in my portfolio, if one was going really badly I often felt less wounded by it thanks to the joy I was drawing from the others. Whenever my work on the jet suit was faltering, I'd recall the successes I was having in my day job, or I'd play with the kids. My life operating on the edges seemed a lot more rewarding as a result.

So Dad's chips were down. And off I went to boarding school in the late 1980s.

I think the decision was made to send me to Queen's College in Taunton because it was a good, open-minded school, but also close to my maternal grandparents at a time when my mum and dad needed help with childcare. It was funded by my grandparents and was at least in part intended to insulate me from the increasing financial and emotional pressures at home. Suddenly there I was, at the age of nine, a fairly sheltered, fairly protected, shy and geeky only child, arriving at a new home with 200 surrogate brothers and sisters. It was quite the culture shock, and matters weren't helped when my lovely grandparents sent a parcel of party food for the entire school to eat, meaning everybody could celebrate, and mock, my tenth birthday shortly after my arrival. It was a hugely embarrassing moment for somebody trying to find his way in such an intense and boisterous environment. And my problems were compounded by the fact I had joined at the start of the spring term, out of sync with my fellow students. Like many kids, I found boarding-school life very tough at first. I even remember sometimes getting up in the night to pee and crying at the urinals, just wanting to go home. But we weren't allowed to go home. In fact, for the first month new students weren't even permitted to call their parents. The people in charge believed in clean breaks; a reconnection with the familial home would only make the detachment process harder. I think they had a point, but I was enduring an early lesson: away from the comfort of the woods and Dad's workshop, the Real World was a pretty tough place.

These days, boarding schools have a certain reputation for salacious behaviour, particularly in the era during which I was a pupil, but that wasn't my experience. Sexual shenanigans were non-existent and drug use was limited to one or two merely rumoured joints of marijuana. Instead the prevalent culture was one of physical high jinks – and when I say physical, I mean the kind of physicality delivered with body blows, wrist burns and good old-fashioned tomfoolery. I soon discovered that to leave your possessions unguarded was a mistake. As soon as somebody's back was turned in the dorm, their 'tuck box', a small chest of personal possessions, could be upended and its innards hurled around the room, along with their shoes, socks, books and anything else that came to hand. The term I would use to describe the vibe of my first year at Queen's College would be *character building*. It taught me something vital, which was how to be robust and self-reliant.

After a few years in the junior school it was time to progress to the senior school, where life wasn't helped by the fact that, alongside a couple of friends, I had been installed – entirely by our own choice, I have to say – in a boarding house entitled School House. It was a section of the school that hadn't taken in any new students for a few years, which as we later learned was the result of some quite lawless GCSE and sixth-form groups that had resided there previously: the school was trying to weed out any bad influences before bringing in a younger, less anarchic bunch of students. There was some overlap, though, and we arrived as the last remnants of what had been a particularly brutal pack of fifteen- and sixteen-year-olds were finishing their final year before heading into A-Levels. It soon became apparent that we had entered into a period of our education that could be quite fairly categorized as the Wild West. Mob rule was in place. Occasionally at night, once the dormitory lights had gone out, there would be a brief interlude of peace and calm before the door to our room was flung open. We were sometimes ordered to parade or encouraged to fight one another, purely for the entertainment of the older kids. At other times, an unfortunate victim would protest vainly as several physically stronger and much older boys told him to thread his arms and legs through the steel bunk-bed ladder. The ladder would be detached, but being told to spend the night embracing the cold, hard object was an unenviable punishment – albeit quite a funny one until you were on the receiving end.

I'm aware these high jinks, a *Beano*-style regime of shock and awe, probably sound appalling to some people, particularly today when such behaviours and institutions are rightfully under public scrutiny, but this really wasn't as bad as it might sound, and most of my memories are fond ones. As a thirteen-year-old boy few things are funnier than watching the sixth form presiding over evening homework but choosing instead to see how many of your dormitory colleagues can fit in the hoover cupboard in the corner of the prep room. Being crushed in with your friends was an uncomfortable but a strangely 'bonding-in-adversity' experience, and far more innocent than it might sound today.

As I grew older and more established at school, there was plenty of fun to be had. A small group of us started rock climbing, and took to scaling the school buildings in the middle of the night. I remember one occasion when we had a very deliberate mission, which involved climbing up through the musty attic structure of the five-storey clock tower before abseiling down to the clock face to affix a big Comic Relief red nose to the hour hand in protest at the slightly stuffy headmaster's decision not to allow any celebrations for the annual fund-raising event – I believe it's the closest I've ever got to political activism. We also caused some controversy when a group of us discovered a stash of old porcelain toilet bowls that had been stored in one of the cellars that were located under the school. Having retrieved them via a series of secret passages at night, we then dispatched them all over the grounds and along the battlements that topped the main building. Our bold display caused a bit of a kerfuffle the following morning when the parents of all the students arrived for the highly prestigious Speech Day. But despite these entertaining moments, I found school to be a bit of an academic struggle. My dyslexia meant that a lot of subjects requiring more than a smattering of literacy skills were quite tricky, though unsurprisingly I revelled in anything that involved the slightest hint of practical science. I was evidently a practical kid.

When the weekends approached, I was occasionally allowed to escape from the overwhelming enormity of boarding-school life for just a couple of days, and I savoured every second of my freedom. Much of these away weekends took place in Sherborne with my grandparents – a wonderful food- and adventure-fuelled thirty-six hours. During those frustratingly brief interludes of bliss I would lose myself in the countryside, lying for hours at a time in the nearby fields and watching nature go by. I was still very comfortable with my own company, and having those introspective periods away from the tribal hubbub of dorm life at Queen's College became a very cathartic experience for me.

It was also during these connecting moments with my grandparents, and occasionally Mum and Dad, that I would pick up a few brief insights into my father's continuing struggles. *There was a trip to America for investment . . . Some of his partners aren't coming through on the business side . . . Mum's working longer and longer hours in the City to pay for the remortgage and it's all getting quite pressurized . . .* And then, eventually, my father stopped coming, before sadly, inevitably . . .

Mum and Dad are splitting up.

The arguing and stress had become too much.

can't recall the exact sequence of how things unfolded, but I clearly remember the day my dad died, though maybe even some of that is wrapped up in False Memory Syndrome – the idea that memories can be altered, or misremembered, and that the recollection of certain events becomes different from the reality. Having said that, I'm fairly confident that what I'm about to tell you is accurate.

I was fifteen years old and one night at school I really didn't sleep very well at all. I woke up with a heavy sense of foreboding and dread, as if something bad was happening. I wasn't sure exactly what it might be, so once the morning arrived I tried to shrug it off, quickly getting on with my day. I was in a Physics lesson that afternoon, a course that had become my favourite subject, and with my favourite teacher too: a shy, vulnerable but very interesting guy called Mr Stephens, who always struck me as not being like a regular member of staff at Queen's College in that he was very approachable, and ever so slightly sensitive. If ever anybody messed around during one of his lessons he always looked mortified, as if a personal insult had been hurled from the back of the room.

When our housemaster, Mr Bell, walked into the class to confer with Mr Stephens, no one else thought anything was wrong – it was common for another teacher to briefly interrupt lessons in order to

107

pass on a memo, or instruction. But it was the look on both men's faces that caught my attention. They were panic-stricken, distinctly uncomfortable, and as something was whispered into Mr Stephens' ear his eyes frantically scanned the room before landing nervously, painfully on . . .

Me.

My heart sank. I knew then that either I was about to be accused of some significant misdemeanour – which would have meant a scary fate, to my mind – or a terrible event had taken place at home.

Mr Bell approached me nervously, then asked me to gather my things and follow him out.

I could sense the whispering from my classmates as I left. They were all thinking the same thing: *What's he done? This'll be bad . . .*

Once I'd joined Mr Bell in the corridor, he guided me, confusingly, towards his private accommodation in the school grounds, making several awkward attempts at polite conversation as we walked, knowing that imminently somebody was about to deliver news that would break my heart. That somebody was my mother.

'She's here,' said Mr Bell, ushering me into his lounge. 'There's some difficult news . . .'

While all these events were stacking up in my mind as definitely not being a good thing, nobody mentioned my father at all. *But I knew.* Mum didn't have to say anything. In fact she didn't even discuss the facts of his passing, even as we drove to my grandparents' home together, the pair of us contemplating the horror of what had happened and the uncertainty of our immediate futures. *Dad had ended it all.* It was only later that afternoon when, almost as a formality, she asked if I knew what was wrong that I told her I understood. It was true as well: I *did* understand, I *did* know what had happened, even though nobody had explicitly explained the tragic events of the previous evening to me. I had such a strong connection with Dad, a man I loved and admired and idolized deeply, that I was in full possession of the facts. It was so strange.

The following days and weeks have since become muddied by time, but there are fragments I can recall. I know I became almost unemotional. Mum was quite upset with me because I wasn't expressing any visible pain, but in my head I'd decided there was no point. My thinking was clear.

Look, it's done. I kind of knew we were heading for this. And in a weird way it makes logical sense to me because I'm similar to Dad. I can see that he'd got to such a low point. I'm utterly distraught that it's happened, but . . . I understand.

My mother, on the other hand, was understandably deeply affected. I've since learned that if two people are struck by the same tragedy, and one of them is expressing a lot of grief, there's almost no room for the other person to show any. Their pain gets crowded out. And what was I supposed to do? Have a competition with Mum over who could cry the most? I just knew I had to be there for her.

Away from home I became distant, adolescent and practical about the tragedy. I knew I wasn't going to achieve anything by falling apart. Almost within hours of learning the exact details of my father's passing I'd felt this Y-junction opening up ahead of me. I had been presented with two options. One: I could emotionally collapse into myself, play the victim, and then self-destruct in a horrible fashion. Or two: I could suck it up, realize life isn't fair and learn from the situation. Given those two stark realities, I chose the latter.

'Screw this,' I thought. 'I'm going to grow from here. There's simply no point torturing myself, or sticking metaphorical pins into my eyes. I need to armour up and take on the world – go on and live out all the stuff that Dad would have wanted to do, or wanted *me* to do.'

I'm sure Mum, and a number of other people close to me at school, were probably of the same mind: that I was in denial, or running away from the problem. There was even an attempt at counselling when my housemaster asked if I'd like to chat to the school chaplain. I reluctantly agreed, and together we talked through a lot of emotional issues over the course of an hour or so. But when he then enquired if I'd like to visit his office again, I shrugged him off. I already knew the direction in which life's currents were steering me – and I wanted to get on with it.

Workshop Notes

LIFE ISN'T FAIR

Dad's passing taught me that life can kick you where it hurts – and *hard*. But a lot of innovators and start-up founders don't learn this lesson until it's too late. Tragedy strikes; the best-laid plans fail. Unexpected financial hiccups derail projects. Revolutionary ideas get beaten to the punch by a rival working on the exact same thing. Market values shift. *Shit happens.* Just think of how many businesses went under during the financial crash of 2008 – an event totally out of their control. I know of people who have lost close friends and family members in unpleasant circumstances, but have subsequently found strength in the perspective these events have given them. One of these recently lost their firm a lot of money over a trading deal, but the stresses of that experience paled in comparison to the personal tragedy they had already endured.

There's a propensity to believe we're owed something, or that there's a natural bias or deviation towards things being fair and reasonable. Therefore it's easy sometimes to sit back in the face of our latest misfortune and wonder why life has dealt us such a horrible hand. But that's the opportunity to learn and grow and get stronger as a result. I did that literally after Dad's death, through strenuous exercise and challenges that pushed me away from my comfort zone. It became a positive way of learning from something that might ordinarily have derailed me.

Takeaways

○ Build up your life portfolio. Invest time in sport or hobbies, family activities, a side hustle idea, work goals and so on. If one starts to go wrong, find solace in the things that are going right.

○ Tragedy strikes unexpectedly in business as much as it can in life. It does us good to remember that life isn't fair. We have to roll with the punches rather than fall to the deck at the first blow.

7

GREY SKY THINKING

Or, How Small Problems Can
Lead to Interesting Innovations

There's a quote from the innovator and speaker Stephen Shapiro, author of several bestselling books and speaker on the TEDxNASA talks series, that reads: 'If necessity is the mother of invention, then laziness is sometimes its father.' Shapiro then went on to cite Clifford Berry, builder of the first digital computer in 1930: 'Why did he do this? He said, "I was too lazy to calculate and so I invented the computer."'

But hard work always comes afterwards. Having asked the question, 'There has to be a better way . . .', a person then has to beaver away on their new plan or idea. And once the first project has worked, that becomes a highly addictive process: a buzz always accompanies seeing a new idea through to the end. I believe Steve Jobs and Bill Gates have both been driven by a similar thing. *What if I can build a personal computer? What if we can then advance that technology to a point where it fits in our pocket? What if we can move out of the garage and sell to more people?* There's a reassuring sense of self-belief that comes from success, the ego trip of being able to say, 'I've done that!' And then there's a hunger for more adventure.

To start that ball rolling for ourselves, however, we must first find something that's making life a little too hard, before creating something to improve it. From there, the innovator's journey can begin. My own path started when I decided to find a better way for myself in the wake of Dad's passing: to shut out the psychological pain, I began to physically thrash myself and discovered one or two challenges of my own to overcome through innovation.

Up until that moment I hadn't been a particularly sporty kid, despite my love of the great outdoors. I wasn't great at team activities such as rugby and football, and I tended to do my exercise alone, in nature – walking for hours, stalking rabbits, or mountain biking in the woods close to home. I also never felt the need to compete with other friends. Boarding school had toughened me up for sure, though I didn't want to physically test myself against mates. But once Dad had gone, almost overnight I became self-aware. By that I don't mean I was an insecure kid, awkward, listening to Morrissey records and crying myself to sleep. Instead I located a strong inner confidence. I quite liked the person I was becoming and I knew I had bucketloads of mental fortitude. How? Well, life had punched me right in the balls by snatching Dad away, but I was still standing, surviving. My armour plating had thickened, and the only way to release any pent-up frustrations I had with the world was to unleash hell upon myself, usually during any number of challenges that required large amounts of muscular and mental resilience.

Within a year I'd started rock climbing, overcoming a long-held fear of heights. I was running, too, something I'd spent a childhood avoiding. I began kayaking and would later, briefly, race canoes in Canada for the British Army. Meanwhile, I pressed ahead with my studies – Maths, Physics, and Design and Technology at A-Level. I've listed those subjects in reverse order of enjoyment: I loved nothing more than spending hours making stuff in the school's workshop, turning designs into real things; I hated learning arbitrary rules like calculus in Maths with a passion; Physics was somewhere in the middle, because its mathematics – the formula for dropping an apple on the ground – had a practical purpose. I could visualize the relationships and derive a logic from their application.

Around this time a good friend of mine since our first days at junior school called Lewis and I started taking an interest in the military. Lewis had his own challenging family history and also knew what it was like to feel the absence of a father, so for all sorts of reasons we clicked. Maybe it was that shared lack of a paternal role model, or it was just a male adolescent thing, but we both fixated on pushing ourselves in every testosterone-fuelled environment we could think of.

After three Duke of Edinburgh's Awards, numerous self-organized Brecon Beacons and Scottish Highland expeditions, and even the famous Ten Tors race across Dartmoor, the military felt like a natural progression.

So with much trepidation I attended the Army Regular Commissions Board and after a very stressful couple of days' assessment I was awarded a place to start Officer Training at Sandhurst. But only after completing a decent degree. I landed on a combined Mechanical & Electrical Engineering course at Cardiff University, ideally placed near the mountains and coast, with a great University Officers' Training Corps (UOTC) unit.

I lasted the first term before switching to an Exploration Geology course because I had become so disillusioned, having sat through twenty-three hours of lectures a week during which I learned about stressed beam calculations and yet more calculus. I'd heard that Geology was more hands-on; it seemed more my sort of thing. So I switched courses but had to wait for the remainder of my year to play out because, thanks to the university's rules, I had to start my new degree at the beginning of the following year rather than immediately. This gave me time to have something of an unexpected gap year, during which I worked as a labourer and immersed myself in the UOTC.

In writing this book I've had to analyse some of my motivations and the decisions made in my younger years. I was definitely drawn to the military world because I loved the idea of people pushing their boundaries. I've always enjoyed meeting members of the Special Forces, fighter pilots, individuals who thrive in the extremes of life. It's the same with people who set up and achieve in the world of small business. I like it that a person can enter into an environment that takes them very much out of their comfort zone and succeed, against the odds, during what is usually a very challenging period in someone's life. That appeals to my imagination, probably because of what happened to me in my teens, a time when I was being overwhelmed by the idea that my father was on the cusp of achieving something fantastic, only for it to fail at the last and end badly – very badly. These days there's a part of me that sometimes wonders if I'm actually on a hamster wheel of challenges. I do tend to take on things that might seem incredibly difficult to people around me and draw great pleasure from seeing them through to the end, because somewhere deep in my brain I believe that as a result of completing the latest battle with adversity everything will be OK. *The heartbreak of my youth might be undone.* I've also wondered if the military – and people operating at any elite level, exploring what is humanly possible – has appealed to me because the individuals involved represent inspirational paternal figures. That could be one psychologist's interpretation of my joining the Officers' Training Corps as a student when most of my friends were downing beers and dancing to Britpop in the union bar.

In the dead months before starting my Geology degree I worked my way through what was called the Army's Adventurous Training Course Book, which listed a wide range of challenges that fell under the military's list of appropriate activities and personal accomplishments. I became a rock-climbing instructor, a whitewater-kayaking instructor, competed in canoeing events (that racing gig in Canada), and joined a regular infantry unit's shooting team. I even took up paragliding in Bavaria. Because I was under the British Armed Forces' umbrella, all of these pursuits were free. In some cases I was even paid a few quid for taking part. I couldn't believe my luck.

My mother seemed fairly unfazed by the news that I'd passed the entry tests required to join the military, and was altogether proud and supportive. I think she had adopted the strategy of not trying to dissuade me, knowing it might only heighten my enthusiasm for the idea. Like most kids, once an idea was deemed out of bounds by a parent, I found it took on a more appealing quality. Some people who knew the family story might have thought that I was making a rash and reckless decision, an unwieldy rod for my own back, but subconsciously I felt an atmosphere of sympathy towards my ambitions. It was as if people were saying to me, 'Oh gosh, it must be awful, you must be so hurt, no wonder you want to run away to the military.' That almost enhanced my opportunities in a sense because nobody was going to stop me from doing what I wanted to do because of my father's death.

If, during those first hellish few months, I'd decided that I couldn't cope with school for a month, no one would have batted an eyelid. Had I wanted to be alone for a year, very few people would have mustered the tough love to stop me. I guess I had a certain degree of emotional clemency so Mum, while she probably would have loved to wrap her only son up in cotton wool, adopted the stance that any right-thinking parent would when their tantrum-prone child announces they're running away to join the circus: they offer to pack the sandwiches for what will undoubtedly be a long and arduous journey, all the while praying their kid doesn't actually make it past the first street. But perversely, that hands-off attitude only hardened my resolve. It's probably fair to say that the less interest Mum appeared to take in my ambitions, the more I wanted to prove I was capable of going through with them. She was damned if she did, damned if she didn't.

It was hard work sometimes, though. On paper I was well suited to the pace of military life, as I'd already completed the three stages of the Duke of Edinburgh's Award in sixth form, a programme that encouraged kids to develop a series of self-improvement skills, many of which were learned outdoors. The most exciting part was the Expedition section, where candidates had to plan, prepare and train for an adventure in the UK or, for those who could afford it, abroad. The Gold level was even more thrilling, as it culminated in a residential course that involved a fair amount of living, and playing, in the wilderness, building camps and starting environmentally responsible fires – not too dissimilar to some of the military exercises I would later go on to do, minus the blank rounds, smoke grenades and yelling. And while the Gold expeditions were sometimes fairly arduous, especially when the Dartmoor wind and rain took their toll, it only bolstered my belief that I could cut it in the Army. Once I'd started

my weekly training at the local military base at Maindy Barracks, a requirement for anyone attending the Officers' Training Corps, I found the fitness and field work familiar territory, although Drill, learning to march about in formation, was a trauma.

By the time I'd started my Geology course at the age of nineteen I had met my now wife, Debbie, and my social calendar too was busy. The military schedule required me to attend a drill night every Wednesday, where I would pull on the carefully ironed kit and march about on parade before sitting down for an evening of lectures and tutorials. Every other weekend I would have to attend the barracks to pack my equipment for a couple of days on the Sennybridge Training Area in Wales, a vast area of harsh terrain and windswept hills, which is the same region where most of the Special Forces begin the infamous Selection programme – a vigorous training process designed to spotlight the most battle-ready candidates, the blokes able to cut it in the Special Air Service or Special Boat Service: the best of the best. Luckily, the expectations of the UOTC were not as high. Given that we were university students, the military's top brass had no desire to crush our enthusiasm with the realities of a life in combat. But by the time I'd returned to base in a four-tonne truck a couple of days later, having cleaned my kit before heading back to Cardiff for another week of lectures, I was always wiped out.

I reached another important milestone around the time of joining university: very quickly, my attitude towards the adult figures in my life seemed to flip. I was transformed from a kid into a grown-up. It's a metamorphosis that happens to all of us over time. We look at our parents and understand that they're fallible; we think, 'Oh, you're . . . *just like me.*' And beyond that it's possible to look at the achievers and leaders in the world and confide to yourself, 'Maybe you're not so special. I wonder if I could do that if I really wanted to.' We come to understand that the innovators, creative thinkers and visionaries of this world are just people like us. Granted, they have a few more notches of experience and know-how, but they too started out operating on a level playing field in terms of raw capabilities. Given the same resources, tools and opportunities to compete – such as a similar education, financial status, lucky breaks, and so on – most of us would have a shot at making it in that realm too, if we really put our minds to it.

For a large number of people, that realization happens gradually: our worldview changes with life experiences. We might go away with friends for our first holiday; we meet new people with differing backgrounds at work or university; we buy our first house, our first car; we start our own business. Mistakes happen, people get hurt. We experience triumph and tragedy. After passing a series of emotional waymarkers we come to realize that adulthood and its opportunities and responsibilities are graspable rather than otherworldly fantasies. I was primed for the understanding of that concept when I was fifteen and had all my life experiences banged into my veins in a single hit when Dad died. With hindsight it was a massive overdose of maturity that could have sent me one of two ways: on the path to becoming a self-destructive individual, or a rather obsessively driven, restless thinker with too much energy and ambition for his own good.

Luckily, in that 50/50 toss my coin landed the right way up.

And then along came my first-ever innovation . . . the Head-Over.

When I was studying at Cardiff University, the psychology among most people in their final year seemed to be quite relaxed when it came to what might follow graduation. It said: *If I can just get a 2:1 degree, or even a First, there's bound to be a conveyor belt of amazing jobs waiting for me on the other side.* There was little thought of gaining real work experience, or signing up for an undergraduate scheme of some kind. I watched as friends from my engineering course, all now a year ahead of me, were heading out of the university system and learning very quickly that the nation's employers couldn't really give two craps about their long-term ambitions of opening a tea shop in Patagonia, or working from Madrid as a documentary maker. When this reality inevitably bit, seeking out employment became a very disheartening experience for some mates of mine. The fallout was that a number of them abandoned their pipe dreams and were considering their next steps into adulthood. Some decided to travel for a year or so, hoping the world might soften its attitude in the interim. Others signed up to teacher-training schemes. Not for the first time I realized I wanted to set myself apart from the crowd, and in a big way.

My first plan was to set up a small start-up of my own, gaining some semblance of work experience during my second year which I felt might give me a head start come graduation day. During my adventures with the Officer Training Corps, I had stumbled across an idea for an interesting piece of kit called the Head-Over – a tube of fleeced material that a soldier (or builder, or student waiting for the bus) could pull around the neck, or over the head, to keep warm. A bungee drawstring was connected to the top, making it possible to tighten one end to make a beanie hat, trapping any heat inside. Effectively it was an early version of a snood before snoods became mainstream, gaining popularity among the cold-averse blokes plying their trade in the Premier League.

I'd first imagined the design during one particularly miserable weekend trudging around in the pouring rain on the Brecon Beacons. I was rather disappointed by the rudimentary nature of our Army issue kit. It all seemed so completely outdated: there were cotton jackets, cotton trousers, cotton *everything*. We were often cold, and rarely was anything waterproof – mainly because waterproof clothing tended to rustle loudly, which was considered unacceptable from a tactical perspective. As a result, everybody was prone to getting and staying wet for hours on end, which only added to the chill factor. Given my tendency to dream and fantasize about design ideas, I figured that an item of clothing such as the Head-Over could improve the situation significantly, and at low cost, given its shape and size.

'It would be a bit like putting a scarf on,' I said, explaining the concept to one friend while we 'bivvied up' on an exercise. 'It would stop the hot air escaping from your jacket, or top. You can pull it on and off again quickly, and tighten a drawstring to close the end and turn it into a beanie, even hiding it under your helmet. All-round it's a really neat piece of kit.'

This elevator pitch couldn't have been better timed. With the rain dripping down our backs, and my friend shivering in the cold, I had made the Head-Over's very first sale.

I made a small run of half a dozen and, to my surprise, I located several other interested parties almost immediately, mainly friends from the UOTC. The profits, while not being anything to write home about, were enough to cover the Head-Over's next round of material costs. I was probably making two or three pounds on each item, not accounting for my labour. This next run was snapped up incredibly quickly, and my profit margins created a healthy income, helped by the fact that Cardiff was enduring something of a brutal freeze at the time, and soldiers tend to notice when another 'oppo' has a new piece of kit that makes their existence slightly less miserable.

It didn't take many weekend exercises before my Head-Over was one of the winter's must-have items. In fact my orders list was so large that within weeks I was knocking on the doors of friends, and friends of friends, desperate for anyone with sewing machine expertise to help me piece together another box of garments. I handed over yards of pre-cut fleece material and draw cords, paying my new fleet of seamstresses for every item they produced as my trading results went up and up. I even supplied the Head-Over to several UOTC units around the country, having had the idea to send a free one to the head of each training unit. It turned out one officer had a day job running a motorcycle school, and put in an order for several hundred. A whole new market of cold-necked motorists I hadn't thought of. Sure, my work wasn't going to make me an overnight millionaire, but the project did give me a massive head start when launching myself into a lifetime of innovation: I was at least able to demonstrate the type of go-get-'em attitude that potential employers loved to hear about during job interviews.

And that's exactly where I was heading next.

As I headed towards the long summer break of my second year I'd heard that BP were looking to recruit a crew of undergraduates for an internship-style scheme. Within it, the brightest and best could expect to earn a £20,000 pro rata salary for three months of summer work. In the meantime they would scoop up all the experience an eager mind could handle. I loved the idea, though there was an understanding that I was up against it in terms of selection. The calibre of student BP were looking to recruit was typically high-end; the Oxbridge genius type. Given that I was a Geology student from Cardiff with a sideline in fashion retail and military adventure, I wasn't so confident of making the grade, but that didn't put me off.

I applied regardless, and having passed an assessment I was granted an interview, where my first thought was to wax lyrical about my Head-Over project. It certainly ticked all the boxes for a listening assessor: to their mind I was a creative self-starter who had spotted a gap in the market; all distribution hurdles had been overcome and I'd managed my costs and margins with aplomb. I was quickly enrolled on the programme, where I found myself working for BP Retail in the slightly less-than-glamorous environs of Milton Keynes. Not that I cared too much. I had my first desk job and was earning what felt like a bucketload of cash. Then, towards the end of an enjoyable three months, an opportunity came up to visit the oil trading floor in London.

The drama of the place was an experience like no other. Located in London's Lehman Brothers building, the space buzzed with an energy every bit as thrilling as the Hollywood dramatization of a stock exchange, as evidenced on films such as *Trading Places*. Having been invited to witness trading for myself, I watched transfixed by what seemed to be organized chaos masquerading as work. The floor was L-shaped, open-plan, with around 500 people jammed inside. There wasn't a suit to be seen, and the age demographic was much younger than any office I'd stepped into before. At certain moments the energy of the trading floor surged; people jumped up with the stereotypical phone handset jammed under their chin, waving their hands and shouting at other members of the tightly bunched team. There were demands for shipping information, prices and order confirmations. Nobody stood idly at the coffee machine chatting about their golf weekend. A permanent buzz seemed to hang around this place. There were whispers that somebody had booked a big deal before breakfast and the company's notable personalities were pointed out to me as we toured the floor, most of them described in near mythical terms.

I had stepped into an exciting new world.

Becoming a part of it was my new focus.

Shortly afterwards I was back in Cardiff for my final year, where I tripped over boxes of fleece materials and elasticated cords, the Head-Over business still ticking over nicely, while I pushed determinedly towards a full-time job with BP. I hoped to secure a place on their much-lauded Formal Graduate Scheme, a placement for anyone with the grades and chutzpah to compete in what was a cut-throat business. I knew that my previous experience with the company, plus the enterprise shown by my Head-Over creation, stood me in good stead as I completed the relevant assessments and tests. I networked in my downtime and then networked some more, until eventually I was ushered through the portals of acceptance into the alpha environment of the trading floor of one of the biggest oil companies in the world. At the age of twenty-two, I had landed my first post-university position, right in the thick of it.

While being rotated in various roles on the Formal Graduate Scheme over those three years from 2001 to 2004, I was able to cling to the excitement of the oil-trading game, which was where I'd decided I wanted to end up, especially having discovered some of the pay scales on offer. The numbers were mind-boggling to me, and typically those people working at the top end of the pay scale had the egos to match their bank balances. I had the sense that I was somewhat outside that crowd, though. The big personalities were uber confident, aggressive alpha male types – including the women. I worked hard to fit in, but I didn't have the temperament or the desire to compete on their terms.

I knew that to succeed in that environment I would have to operate in another way – *my way*.

Workshop Notes

WRITE A NARRATIVE FOR YOURSELF

Stories resonate with people. It was the way we communicated and shared ideas with one another long before the written word was even invented. Our brains are nicely tuned to work with stories, especially if they have a clear beginning, middle and end. The story of an idea, a discovery, a battle, a struggle, success and failure are all appealing narratives, and creating one for yourself can set up future successes when building a business or project that you're trying to sell to investors, future employers or collaborators.

The Head-Over was my first story. I had stumbled across an idea, followed through with research and development, overcome the doubters, jumped the hurdles and carried a successful prototype over the line. As we shall see, the narrative created a strong reputation for me within BP and beyond, opening doors to different opportunities in the future. It also propelled me along a path to a point where I now run an international jet suit business.

An interesting story of creativity or adventure is a great way to show our drive to the world.

Now create your own.

Takeaways

○ We are predisposed to respond to narratives; people we might need to influence in the future can be swayed by their power. We should ensure to build an interesting backstory for ourselves by attempting to innovate and create in our own time. Even stories of failure can be helpful, sometimes more so than experiences of success.

○ Find an interesting area to create in. The Head-Over turned out to be a great experiment, and a valuable learning experience. It was also a simple fix to an annoying problem. We can always innovate by looking at the things that make our lives difficult and working to improve them. Laziness is the father of invention.

○ We should always strive to learn from the people ahead of us in the queue, as I did at BP. No matter what industry we work in we should watch, pick up the tricks of the trade, and figure out how best to improve them.

THE MAGPIE SPIRIT

Or, How to Press Ahead in Moments of Self-doubt

t's easy to dismiss an unusual idea, to say, 'This will never work.' And to have those same words aimed at us is a dispiriting experience. As I worked on the jet suit, I found it to be quite a lonely journey. At times it was as if I was walking a pathway peppered with signposts that read 'Don't Be Stupid!' or 'Beware: Your Career Will Die Here!' The self-doubt was huge at times.

A lot of business, self-help and innovation books suggest there's a magic formula we can use to overcome these moments, one that delivers endless reserves of Positive Mental Attitude. But that isn't the case. However, to understand that every story of successful innovation contains chapters of insecurity and failure should be enough to tell us that perseverance is rewarded and that mistakes can lead to lessons which, eventually, deliver huge rewards.

My own moments of personal uncertainty and failure could fill an entire book, but I've usually managed to find just enough self-belief to press on regardless, often because I've believed in the strength of my idea, or concept. This was very much in evidence while making my way at BP, where I suppose you could say that I stood out. I had jammed my way into the industry with an interesting anecdote about inventing a piece of useful clothing, but I certainly wasn't the privileged genius type the company could have been accused of favouring in the past. Socially, I also seemed very different from everybody I worked alongside, a fact that was obvious to me from the outset. In what was a young man's game, I had already married. Debbie and I were planning on moving further away from London, having moved to be near work after we had graduated, and into the countryside where we wanted to start a family, which would have been considered a little unfashionable among my peers. Many traders were living it up in fancy City apartments, partying and generally having a whale of a time as single blokes with plenty of cash to splash around. But I was wired differently, in part because of my childhood experience. I really didn't want to take any big financial risks, or make a reckless decision that might impinge upon my personal life.

Even the thought of spending beyond my means, or not having some kind of a financial plan in place, made me nervous. Were I to make it as a trader, I had to learn to take managed risks when working with the company's money or resources. As I began to find my way at BP on the Graduate Scheme I noticed that some of the people working around me thrived on the gambling aspect of the enterprise. The stressful adventure of walking the knife-edge between success and failure brought them to life. I'd previously experienced that same feeling whenever I took on a physical challenge, something arduous such as a long-distance race, and later ultra-marathons, where the exertions were confined to just physical pain and mental resolve rather than anything that could threaten my home life. The endorphins bounced around for hours afterwards. At the weekends, in my early BP years, I often returned from gruelling long runs and cycle rides, my body fatigued and mentally drained, but the suffering was self-contained. There was no risk to the pay cheque that put a roof over our heads, so there was a safety net there, one that had been constantly threatened as I grew up. I wasn't getting my kicks from taking any financial risks at home. My physical challenges seemed so much more doable than me saying to Debbie, 'I've just come up with a great business idea and I'm going to drop everything to pursue it. It might make us a fortune, or it might ruin the family. Fingers crossed!' I simply wasn't able to live with the possibility of a negative outcome. Worst-case scenarios worried me too much.

As I settled into my career, I knew that, given my personality, I had two options if I was to thrive in what was clearly a cut-throat, aggressive industry. The first was to connect with a 'book leader', a senior trader, doing my time as their junior analyst, then junior trader, for five or six years until they eventually retired, or were poached by another firm. I might then be in pole position to inherit all the fruit of our labours, having learned the tricks of their trade. Option two was to come up with an innovative idea or process within the game, a moment of genius that catapulted me into a more senior position on merit. I knew sucking up to other traders for several years wasn't really for me because following boring procedure, or moving with the crowd, was deeply unmotivating and frankly something I wasn't very good at. Instead I decided to locate a niche angle for myself within BP, a useful role that could be expanded into something more lucrative further down the line. But how to engineer such a breakthrough?

I was always on the lookout for an angle others might have missed, that twinkle of an opportunity that just might yield a big result, against the odds. It's not easy keeping faith that such a chance will present itself. But then it did.

At some point in the early stages of my career I attended a meeting where several traders were discussing a new technology. Apparently, a line of software had been developed to reduce collisions on the numerous shipping routes criss-crossing the oceans, and the news had been picked up by BP Shipping's health and safety community. Despite being a fringe issue for most traders, the concept of anti-collision procedures was a hot-button topic for companies such as BP, not least following the horrors of the *Exxon Valdez* disaster of 1989. In what has since been regarded as one of the worst ever man-made calamities, an oil tanker owned by the petroleum company Exxon – then one of the so-called Seven Sisters, the group of companies that ruled the oil industry – ran aground on the Prince William Sound's Bligh Reef, just off the coast of Alaska. Some 10.8 million gallons of crude oil leaked into the sea, and the story dominated the media for weeks. The spill eventually extended across 11,000 square miles of ocean and 1,300 miles of coastal land.

By the time of my arrival, BP's thinking was clear: nobody wanted to repeat an avoidable catastrophe of the kind made infamous by the *Exxon Valdez*. From a business perspective, Exxon had nearly collapsed following the incident. Lord Browne, the head of BP, had worked through that sticky period by forming BP Shipping, where the focus on health, safety and the environment was intense. To gain even more control over how the job was done, BP Shipping decided the company should ship 40 per cent of their oil and oil products themselves, rather than contracting the job out to other freight companies.

To most people, talk of health and safety and anti-collision technology didn't sound like the sexiest project in the world. However, it was the underlying concept of gaining a commercial insight into ship voyages that sparked my interest. I had a sense it might lead towards the sort of peripheral opportunity I had been searching for.

t turned out the meeting was pretty dull. Yet I left feeling intrigued by this new navigational system. In layman's terms, the technology comprised a radio-frequency transmitter and receiver that alerted captains and coastguards to any passing traffic within their ship's immediate vicinity. The basic plan was to stop ships from hitting one another in fog, or busy shipping lanes, as the system pinged out the location of a vessel, plus its speed and bearing, on a communication that could be picked up by any boat carrying the right equipment. The system was called the Automatic Identification System (AIS) and differed to standard radar, a passive system that locates vessels by hitting them with radar signals, instead receiving more accurate data actively transmitted by each ship. Simply by glancing at a monitor, all commercial shipping captains would be able to understand the exact locations and movements of everybody around them at any given time.

The International Maritime Organization mandated that every large commercial vessel was to be fitted with the technology. This ruling was universally considered a good thing, as it would prevent ships from banging into one another in the middle of the ocean, spilling their cargoes into the fragile ecosystems beneath and costing firms a great deal of money in losses.

My imagination, the part of my brain that couldn't help but ponder the imponderables, was fired up by the news.

Did this tech have some other use?

The answer, as I discovered quite quickly, was yes, it did. The otherwise dull meeting had yielded some interesting information at the very end: the system was 'free to air' and unencrypted, meaning the data transmitted by each ship could be collected by a receiver positioned on the shoreline. With the right tech, it was then possible to listen to all the ships moving around a coastal region as they pinged out directions and speeds at a frequency of every ten seconds; all the vital stats regarding a moving vessel could then be relayed to anyone needing to track that ship – if they were able to access the data, that is.

My mind was racing. What else was possibly contained in this stream of data? After some follow-up investigation I struck gold. Not only was each ship sharing its live position, heading and speed, but to my astonishment part of the message contained a declaration of the ship's intended destination and its estimated time of arrival. Despite my junior position I knew enough about the trading business to spot that this could be hugely insightful and valuable. I knew that if data of this kind were laid out on a digital map, BP's traders could observe the movements of every oil-carrying ship on the water, and accurately predict trade flows. If that were the case, I might have found the niche angle I was looking for: through innovation I'd present a massive tactical advantage over our rivals, not just for my team but for numerous BP trading benches around the world.

But the idea was almost too simple, and too obvious, so naturally I began to question the validity of my breakthrough. I was confused as to why nobody at BP had thought of it before, especially given the high value of possessing that kind of knowledge when everybody within the trading game was always looking to maximize any such tactical gains.

My fears were initially well founded when I attempted to share my vision. To my surprise the response was noncommittal, maybe even indifferent. In fact nobody seemed the slightest bit interested.

'That sounds like a waste of time,' shrugged my boss when I first told him. 'I'd really just carry on with the day job.'

Was I overlooking something? I sensed real value in this ship location information, so undeterred I badgered my boss until eventually he relented. I was to do all the research on my own time. And in no way was it to interfere with my actual job. But I had his blessing and a modest budget with which to explore the idea.

I worked furiously for several months. My first challenge was to find a way of collecting all the data shared between ships on a series of land-based receivers. I'd learned that Lloyd's of London had instructed one of their technical divisions to experiment with distributing subsidised AIS antennas in return for recipients pooling their data feeds. Many were actually hobbyists, not too dissimilar to train-spotting enthusiasts, but instead of gathering at the end of Euston Station with pads and pens, they tended to meet in places such as Poole Harbour with their binoculars. I'd been told that most ship-spotters simply noted the names of every ship that passed, but now, equipped with receivers kindly donated by Lloyd's of London, their game had been upgraded considerably. Suddenly anyone interested was able to collect the all-important IMO (International Maritime Organization) number of a passing vessel, giving them access to all sorts of other specifications and data online.

In 2004 the internet, while up and running with the likes of Ask Jeeves and MySpace, was still an industrial tool-in-waiting rather than the globe-eating behemoth it is now. But I discovered that the Lloyd's of London team had done a great job with the antenna roll-out. Not only were most of the ports and near-shore shipping lanes covered by enthusiasts and their receivers, each with a range of 30–50 miles, but the data was being captured and had the potential to be displayed on a live feed. But weirdly, Lloyd's seemed almost as oblivious to the potential of their technology as my bosses at BP.

If I was right, it was only a matter of time before another trader or trading analyst, somebody with a little too much thinking time, stumbled across the same thought as me. Speed was of the essence. But I understood that playing it cool was the only way forward. Getting excited in front of Lloyd's, the very people detailing how this new technology worked, would only have alerted somebody there that a really exciting idea was waiting to be discovered.

'There might be some interest from us,' I suggested. 'Could we access the feed of data coming across your network, for free, to see how we might work with it?'

To my surprise, they agreed. I was given access to a pipeline of vital information, feeding live from all over the world. The difficulty was figuring out how to contain it.

I knew I had to find a way to place all this data on an easy-to-understand mapping system, so traders could access their shipping information at a glance, much like Uber customers follow their cars on the app today. I discovered a company called MapInfo; they functioned in a similar way to Google Maps before Google Maps even existed. Their work usually focused on tracing the movements of marked delivery vans, or the occasional lost dog with the help of a homing beacon attached to its collar. I knew their platform might also work on something much larger, such as a map charting the movements of an oil tanker fleet. The thought of linking up with a company as far-reaching as BP excited MapInfo, so I was able to negotiate their support to build a basic modified version of their mapping system. It consumed my entire meagre budget but my prototype was ready.

N ow, if you don't mind, I'd like to briefly pause this story for a second in order to outline just how jet fuel trading, as an example, worked at the turn of the last century. BP was then

operating across Singapore, Chicago and London. A trader working in jet fuel for planes only really cared about supply and demand, which was no different to most markets, and demand was usually fairly easy to comprehend. In Europe, for example, traders knew how busy airlines were at different times of year, and by deploying some maths it was possible to understand just how much fuel a nation would need. The numbers stayed relatively stable, because airlines liked to keep their planes busy. The only times those numbers might vary arrived during a war, which saw an increase in jet fuel for all those fast-moving fighter planes, or a global disaster that affected air travel, such as 9/11 and clearly, at the time of writing, Covid.

Europe refines and produces its own jet fuel, but its output is nowhere near enough to satisfy the demands of those workaholic airlines, so it has to import, typically from the Middle East, from where there used to be three jet fuel cargoes arriving into Europe a month. Prior to the arrival of AIS, in order to track the ships carrying those lucrative loads as they moved out of the Arabian Gulf through the Red Sea, a port agent had to be relied upon to log and count the number of vessels leaving or entering the region. As soon as a company like BP collected that information they were able to better estimate the volume of jet fuel coming into Europe and compare it to the demand, which ultimately affected the market price.

With the help of AIS, the company's traders would have the information they required to make a call on market price direction as soon as tankers left their ports – the results would be immediate. Rather than us waiting several days for some bloke with binos to phone in the numbers, vital details would now be available at the swipe of a mouse. I could watch as traders loaded my improved version of the Automatic Identification System, typing in a search command for their vessels. The mission-critical details of how much fuel was arriving in Europe, and when, were there in front of them, arriving around seven days ahead of their competitors, who were still relying on spotters and notepads. My simple idea had the potential to change the game overnight.

But there was a problem: where to host this new ship-mapping system? The IT department at BP were understandably focused on keeping the existing critical trading systems running. Luckily, I was to find a charitable soul in the company's IT department in South Africa, where a lovely contact of mine offered to host it on the intranet server.

I was in.

Before LinkedIn, Twitter and Facebook, alerting people to your online presence was a little more *beta*. Once everything was in motion, I had no way of advertising my new, experimental resource to BP's info-hungry traders other than to copy out the URL address of my ship-tracking page before printing it out on good old-fashioned A4 paper. I distributed sheets on the BP trading floor in London, with a note that read, simply: 'Live ship tracking intelligence at' followed by the link.

Traders are, by nature, a curious bunch, so I had a hunch this note would be impossible for them to resist. I tried to get on with my day job that morning but caught glimpses of my mapping platform lighting up screens around the office. A couple of senior traders were huddled around one, waving their hands around. It was almost as though I'd walked into the bookies and told them all which horses were going to win that week's races.

Renamed the Global Energy Map, or GEM, this innocent little web portal caused a sensation and spread virally across the company's global trading offices. Whilst not generating money directly it was universally acknowledged for providing key insights that led to a significant revenue increase for the business. I gave up paying too much attention to the numbers, but the effect on the company's working practices had been so significant that everyone was now using GEM.

As you can imagine, with GEM's success stories piling up I was soon confirmed as something of a celebrity: this unknown junior who had developed a game-changing innovation in the global commodity trading arena. My offbeat theory, fleshed out alone, and all for the cost of £30,000, had put me on the map – in more ways than one.

Receiving an invitation to present an idea, or hare-brained scheme, to our mythical CEO Lord Browne and the BP board was unheard of at my level. These chats were typically confined to senior management types, politicians and even heads of state. Lord Browne had quite the reputation within the industry, having overseen what was considered a boom period for BP; he was also a crossbench member of the House of Lords and would later go on to be the President of the Royal Academy of Engineering. During his time at the company he brokered meetings with Libya's Colonel Gaddafi and Russian leader Vladimir Putin. He certainly wasn't one to suffer fools. So it was with some trepidation that I accepted an invitation to present GEM.

In a darkened room, with a PowerPoint presentation running, I explained the thinking behind GEM. I had figured that Lord Browne would be more interested in safety than trading value, so had prepared a visual replay of two collisions we had the positional data for. One was a minor 'exchanged paint' incident involving one of our ships, found not to be at fault. ('Exchanging paint' was a rather quaint way of describing a slight, though nerve-racking, nautical collision.) The second was a tragic incident in the Aegean Sea, where a ship, unrelated to BP, struck an ore carrier. The events were replayed on the GEM system where everything seemed to happen in slow motion. The two vessels in the Aegean, unaware of each other at the time the accident took place, collided and deflected away from each other, before the blinking signal from the iron ore carrier disappeared completely. In real life the vessel had been sunk at a huge cost, but through GEM's simulation it was clear to see how the disasters could have been easily averted, given the new technology provided by AIS.

When the lights came up, there was a pause. Lord Browne seemed to be taking stock of my work. I drew a deep breath. It was as if I'd been dropped into the lion's den.

'For the first time in history,' began Lord Browne – which, I can say from experience, is always a knife-edge way to begin the appraisal of any idea: what follows is either going to be fantastic or downright humiliating – 'we're able to accurately replay shipping incidents. Up until now, the industry has relied on the verbal accounts of survivors after incidents as horrific as the ones detailed here. Richard, this might change the world.'

I was rocked. This was an incredibly flattering thing to say, and I was at pains to point out that I'd simply shown him the work drawn together from several disparate resources: the tracking information of the Automatic Identification System, the transmitters and receivers handed out by Lloyd's, and the map-reading tech of Map-Info. My innovation had been to spot the opportunity and get on with figuring out how to collate these resources while finding some interesting ways to utilize their combined efforts. *But that left-field thinking had worked.* Within weeks we had assembled a proper team to productionize GEM. AIS-based ship tracking systems are now widespread and integrated into every commercial shipping operation globally.

My life was changed too: the belief in going against the grain had been reaffirmed, and in a way that was now addictive. I'd always loved proving my doubters wrong, and it didn't have to take place in a business setting either. When people raised doubts over my extreme physical challenges, I was spurred on. I'm not alone in feeling that way either: people considered too fragile or too old to cope with an adventure often gather inspiration from pessimistic comments. Then there are the countless, deeply romantic tales of sports stars being written off as past their prime only for them to sweep once more to glory, such as Tiger Woods recently.

Personally, I'd always enjoyed the idea that somebody could dismiss a strange new idea of mine as bullshit, only for me to do it anyway, *and for it not to be bullshit.* From a working point of view GEM was exactly that: a weird innovation that was *not bullshit.* But carrying a far-fetched idea over the line and defeating the odds appealed to me immensely. The fact that it resonated with my father's sense of adventure added extra emotional heft. I found GEM's success to be liberating and hugely stimulating.

It hadn't all been plain sailing, however. There were times during the development process when even I had doubted the idea's chances of acceptance. Some nights I returned home and wondered to myself, 'Why am I doing this? I'm gradually digging myself into a hole here.' I feared a nightmarish moment, my £30,000 research project amounting to nothing more than an embarrassing hole in someone's budget. In those moments of doubt I was standing red-faced, the corporate system circling around me, laughing, telling me I'd wasted my time, in an echo chamber of misery.

Luckily, that didn't happen. In fact, thanks to GEM, my reputation and career at BP benefitted hugely. Consider the example of A&R people in the music industry – individuals found at every record label in the world, each one charged with unearthing the next Beyoncé, or Metallica. All day they scour the internet for interesting demos. They listen to SoundCloud cuts and watch YouTube videos; at night, often seven days a week, they're found trawling dive bars and basement clubs hoping to sign an act that ninety-nine times out of a hundred is in no way a match for the hype generated by their social media footprints. It's a thankless task, and the work can be unforgiving on both the ego and the liver, given the amount of drinking that takes place when trying to schmooze the artists that *are* great, who usually, somewhat inevitably, sign for a rival label with a bigger hospitality budget.

However, should somebody land that once-in-a-generation band, an artist that goes on to shift millions of records, headline Glastonbury and sell out a succession of nights at Wembley Stadium; should they sign the next Coldplay, Amy Winehouse or Foo Fighters, it's likely some gold-plated opportunities will then fall into that person's lap. Or at least their failures – the not-so-successful signings that almost certainly follow in the wake of their greatest success – will be forgiven more easily. *Forget the duds: he or she had the golden touch that discovered Tom Jones in a working men's club.* One good example is Nick Huggett, who discovered the platinum-selling singer Adele, who then signed with XL Recordings and was a huge success. 'The difficult thing about signing someone like Adele is finding another one,' Huggett told Q magazine in 2017. 'It's hard to follow up that as an A&R. I don't beat myself up about it.'

GEM was my Adele, and for the next ten years I was given a lot more freedom to pursue unusual or challenging business development or technology project opportunities, all the while being forgiven for any red herring chases because I was the graduate who had pulled together the Global Energy Map. My success had given me free rein to experiment and travel the world, as well as a small spot bonus. More lucratively, it was to shove me towards a place on the fast track into the adrenalized and highly charged world of the oil market, and later, a career as a jet suit pilot.

But first, there was a world of physical suffering still to endure.

Workshop Notes

DON'T BE DISHEARTENED BY DISINTEREST

During GEM's development I went through phases where I believed I'd wasted my time. That seems laughable now, but for a while the fear was almost crushing.

And sometimes pressing ahead regardless can be just as damaging as giving up.

I recently gave a talk at a local grammar school where I explained that there's no true test for knowing when you're travelling a pathway that will end in a good place, or a bad place. Instead, we have to balance our never-say-die attitudes with the humility to acknowledge when we've gone too far with something that isn't going to work. There is no formula that tells us where that point is. No business book, family member or friend can explain exactly when it might arrive. Rather, we have to be at once our own critic and fan, and follow the only true guide we have: *our gut instinct*.

Takeaways

○ Find any opportunity to stand out from the crowd within your industry. As I did with GEM, it's possible to look to areas that some people might find dull or irrelevant and find new ways to innovate within them to great success.

○ Patience is key when innovating. Sometimes ideas catch fire quickly. Others burn slowly and take a while to capture the imagination.

○ Opportunity is everywhere, even in the most boring of meetings.

WAR GAMES

Or, What the Military Taught Me About Persistence

t's quite easy to align the mental requirements of a life in the military, or as an athlete, with the psychological resilience needed to be a successful entrepreneur, or innovator. The similarities are really quite striking.

The British Armed Forces set an admirable standard when it comes to endurance, both mentally and physically. Extreme sporting events such as ultra-marathon running take you into a similar world. You don't have to accept limits; every boundary is there to be challenged. This is a deeply attractive concept to a lot of people for whom going the extra mile has always been a compelling goal. When working through a frustrating problem in the workshop I've often brought to mind the classic British military attitude, as epitomized by war films such as *A Bridge Too Far* and *Battle of Britain*: the sense that no matter how hellish a mission becomes, you stay strong and when you get knocked down you get back up. Then afterwards we'll have a nice cup of tea while making jokes about how bloomin' horrible it all was. A traditionally dry British sense of humour can be an invaluable asset at such times.

That mentality was essential when I was building my start-up, Gravity Industries. There were moments of extreme difficulty, periodic setbacks that threatened to derail the best-laid plans, and flashpoints when quick thinking and decisiveness were vital in order to succeed. On a practical level, many of my successes can be attributed to my education in the military and exposure to extreme physical challenges. I've forged ahead in dark moments when some people might have downed tools and quit. During the early phases of research and development on the suit I spent thousands of pounds on a series of jet turbines, unsure whether my theories on assisted flight were well founded. *Was I wasting my hard-earned money on a dead-end idea?* The self-doubt and pressure were high; walking away and scrubbing off the work as a lost cause seemed the best decision at times. But past experience had told me explicitly, 'You think this is where your limits are – both in the mind and body – but that's not the case. There's always more you can achieve.'

It's true, too.

I pressed ahead with my work when building the suit because experience had taught me I had more to give, especially in those moments when I believed my breaking point was approaching. In 2016, when the research and development stage was only a part-time project, I thrashed my body as I tried again and again to take flight. Engines failed. Control systems failed. Fuel systems failed. I sometimes worked all weekend only to spend a brief second or two in flight. And the crashes, when they happened, were quite painful. But in those brief airborne moments, the pleasure and sense of achievement were consuming and addictive. Like the high-handicap golfer hacking around his or her local course for seventeen holes only to birdie the eighteenth, I was often given a bread-crumb of encouragement to temper my frustrations. It was usually enough to fire me up for another weekend of effort. I was also fortunate enough to have the unrelenting support of Debbie, her father Sam, and a small group of friends, especially software engineer Jon Reece, who kept the faith despite relentless setbacks.

Years before Gravity, with life set on a promising trajectory at BP, and family life feeling settled, I turned my attention once again to what had become of late a neglected pastime: the search for physical self-flagellation. Upon my graduation from university several years earlier I'd reluctantly decided not to accept my place for Officer Training at the Royal Military Academy Sandhurst. I'd spent enough time getting muddy on the Brecon Beacons and I wasn't prepared to abandon my soon-to-be-fiancée to military life. But it was a decision always tinged with regret. I soon missed the camaraderie and battling spirit; I'd loved the sense that I was pushing myself harder than I'd ever done before. So when my final graduate position at BP was converted into a permanent role, I gave in to my masochistic cravings and signed up as a Reservist for the Royal Marines in London.

I remember looking around at various Territorial Army units but it was the Royal Marines that really impressed me and represented the most exciting challenge. They were considered a backfill for regular Commando units and a source of extra manpower – fully trained Commandos who were expected to be as battle-ready as their full-time comrades. I later learned that a number of troops on the ground at certain points during the Coalition's war in Afghanistan were Royal Marines Reservists. I liked the idea that one minute a person could be working at their desk for a company such as Morgan Stanley, or serving customers in the Disney Store, and the next they were being called up to fight for Her Majesty. That was intensely appealing.

A responsibility of the kind instilled by the Royal Marines didn't come easily, though. To make it through as a Reservist, every individual had to train to the exact same specifications as a regular commando – a fact that was impressed upon me from the moment I signed up. At the beginning of my training course I was shouldered by around eighty like-minded blokes, all of them keen to achieve their green berets – the sign of a fully fledged Royal Marine. Two years later, only two of us remained, myself and one other bloke. The attrition rate had been appallingly high, but understandably so. Imagine working your guts out all week in a regular job, and combining that with the physical and mental beasting of a mid-week barracks 'drill night', whilst somehow keeping up a self-motivated training regime – only to then have to drag your exhausted backside to the same barracks on most Friday nights for forty-eight hours of further thrashing in the great outdoors, often with next to no sleep. Our workload was exhausting; motivating myself on those Friday evenings was sometimes the most challenging moment of the week, especially when mates were organizing parties or weekends away, or preparing to relax at home on the sofa in the bosom of their loved ones. It's little wonder the drop-out numbers were so high.

During those weekends away the physical work required to pass out as a Royal Marines Commando was intense. We always arrived on base at night, quickly packing our kit for what would be an extended run throughout the evening, with brief periods of marching. The unit would then 'harbour up' as the sun rose, before running through a range of training drills, later embarking on a night assault at the day's end. Meanwhile, the unit required every individual within it to be physically powerful. Commandos had to be pretty decent long-distance runners, and they needed strength both in the gym and out of it, usually for lengthy yomps in freezing or roasting conditions when we were obliged to carry weaponry and 30lb of typically wet kit.

I soon noticed that it wasn't necessarily the strongest or the fastest blokes that stood out from the rest of the group. Some lads were gym monkeys but couldn't hack the running. Others were big on cardio-vascular power but struggled to bang out the pull-ups, press-ups and weighted rope climbs. Resilience was the overriding trait in demand, as anyone who has endured a military conflict will attest to. But achieving a suitable level of mental and physical toughness required serious effort and the injury rate became a debilitating factor. After two days of drills in the pouring rain, the body begging for rest, it wasn't uncommon for a recruit to snap an ankle or knee ligaments, their heavy standard-issue boots slipping awkwardly in the mud. By Sunday night all of us were broken. I'd wearily pack my bags for home, where there was time for a few hours' recuperation as I prepared for yet another week of joyous office grind. Fighting the fatigue was a 24/7 battle.

What helped me through was a sense of brotherhood, a General Union of Suffering that was shared between the recruits in equal measure. That sense was heightened during times when the pain was overwhelming, the workload never-ending, and our environment unrelenting in its brutality, often when it was icy cold and raining, which tended to happen a lot in the British countryside. The higher-ups weren't complete sadists (though I suspected some of the trainers might be). Rather, the attitude was 'train hard, fight easy'. Worryingly, that gave our trainers free rein to beast the crap out of anyone hoping to join their ranks, and they often drove us into the mud on a Sunday morning as we teetered at our lowest ebbs, having not eaten or slept properly for over thirty-six hours.

On one such occasion I remember our training team thrashing us a little too hard. The unit had been divided into pairs just before lunch-time and ordered to speed-march in twos, our webbing and kit strapped to our backs, heavy SA80 rifles carried by our sides. The instructions had been to run on the flat or downhill stretches of land and speed-walk over the inclines, pumping our arms dramatically as we moved. There were other obstacles in play: we were moving along sand, which shifted unforgivingly under our heavy boots. After two hours of running, my soul was crushed. But it was only just the beginning.

The group had been tasked with a drill lovingly nicknamed 'The Sickener' – a process that would not stop until the last man had dropped to the floor, or home time had arrived. The psychological twist was that nobody ever forewarned us with those details, so the mental challenge became huge. The internal dialogue was more jarring than the actual effort of running as the brain groaned over and over, *Will this ever end?* One by one the lads fell away, literally, their limp bodies thrown into the back of a waiting truck like bags of wet cement. I must say, I found the experience to be a little self-defeating. If you break a person, if you show them their limits in such a way, it's unlikely they'll be able to carry on when faced with a similar moment of adversity. Their brain will almost always quit. It'll say, 'No, I did this last time and failed. *Give up.*' I believe that the trick is to push a person to breaking point, but pull them back from the edge at the very last moment. This allows them to then creep a little further the next time, and a bit more the next, all the while increasing their strength and resolve.

Somehow, despite the pain racking my entire body, I made it through to the end with three other wannabe commandos, including my good friend James – a crazy ginger-haired tree surgeon by trade whose career path would eventually take him towards the Special Boat Service (he served in Afghanistan). Except it wasn't the end. Not really. To put a crappy layer of icing on a very crappy cake, the two remaining pairs were ordered to pause. Staring into the whites of each other's eyes, I sensed something grim was about to take place. My muscles screamed in agony; my mind told me to quit – to leave. I argued with myself about whether to hang in there or to bail. And then our instructor delivered the cruellest stroke.

'Men standing!' he yelled. 'Grab your partner . . . *and lift!*'

My heart sank; my mind raced. This was now madness. 'This is our *Band of Brothers* moment,' I thought, trying to gulp in oxygen, barely able to place one foot in front of the other.

Our training team were free of concerns. 'Run up that bloody hill,' was the order.

Now panting heavily, and through gritted teeth, I heaved James's form on to my shoulders and dragged myself up a steep incline of shifting sand, my legs buckling beneath me. Once I'd reached the crest of the hill and made it down again, it was James's turn. His shoulders took on my weight at such an angle that the pain stabbing my body felt agonizing.

I later learned that 'The Sickener' was a training session devised by the Special Forces with the particular purpose of hardening their operators to a point where they could deal mentally with any outcome, because in war there were always false endings. Battles don't have scheduled beginnings and convenient climaxes; the enemy always hoped to surprise, to shock, and elite soldiers had to be ready for anything. That was logical thinking. In a battle situation, it's easy to believe that you've made it and survived, only for another wave of violence to rush over you. A soldier in that situation would turn into a nervous wreck without the requisite preparation. During Selection, the Directing Staff would dislocate expectation by claiming an exercise had finished only to ambush the unit minutes later. They would lull recruits into a false sense of security by promising a warm cup of coffee around the corner when in reality another five hours of physical suffering was being prepared.

I pushed on to the bitter end.

We finished the exercise minutes later and the calling of time felt like a landmark achievement. My body and mind blurred in a head-spinning buzz. I was proud and elated, maybe even a little high, and I wasn't the only one. By the looks on the faces of the three blokes around me, slumped to the ground, able to communicate only with a knowing glance of mutual respect and pride, the sense of achievement was shared. Our suffering had become a badge of honour.

I felt euphoric.

t took two years of Royal Marines training to reach a point where I was deemed expert enough to collect my green beret, and it was never easy. To pass out, a potential commando has to complete a series of tests, some physical, some practical, and I'm embarrassed to say it took me three attempts before I was able to become a fully fledged commando. Injury scuppered me the first time round, when I ran along an assault course beam and jumped into the infamous cargo netting, an obstacle familiar to anyone who might have watched the TV show *Gladiators* in the 1990s. (If you haven't seen it, imagine a rope netting resembling the rigging of an old Napoleon-era sailing ship.) During the approach I misjudged my angles and 30lb of equipment landed squarely on the tendon that connected my pectoral muscle to the arm, tearing it in two. I was in agony and unable to move on.

For three months I became hell-bent on completing the testing phase as quickly as possible and, unprepared, and in way too much of a hurry, I cut corners on my second attempt. My attitude pissed off the Directing Staff no end. I was thrown off the course with a warning to take the task more seriously next time. I knew I had to steady myself. I was capable of pushing through what was a psychological barrier to success. The rigmarole of process and procedure might have been mind-numbingly dull, but it was something I *had* to do.

The work soon became utter torture, which was unsurprising given I was trying to complete one of the hardest military assessments in the world. But I somehow set aside my pride, executed in the final test at the third stab, and claimed my green beret, thus setting a new personal standard for myself: *I could cut it in one of the military's most well-respected units.* Quite what Dad would have made of it I'm not entirely sure. I'd like to think he would have appreciated my efforts in the outdoors, thinking on my feet while playing with a grown-up version of the air rifle he had once bought me as a kid.

Although I never saw active service, I took so many vital lessons away from my military experience. Chief among them are my resilience and sheer determination never to give up, but it's also been vital to learn how I react under pressure and cope in highly stressful situations. There are all sorts of examples of people who have frozen when confronted with life-or-death scenarios. I've heard about CCTV videos of avalanches and tsunamis where people have stood, rooted to the spot, staring into the face of disaster, unable to move as an onrushing wave or wall of snow crushes them into oblivion. For most people the thought of running or skiing to safety, or quickly finding refuge, is the most natural reaction; for others, the brain crashes like a malfunctioning laptop. Over the years I've developed quite a harshly pragmatic view of the world, and that's given me a practical, slightly unemotional perspective in crisis situations. I'm not a robot, I'd hasten to add. It's just that during events where panicking would be understandable – in business and in life – I've been able to step back and quickly evaluate a situation before making my considered decision.

At times, when accidentally soaring way too high in the jet suit – which has happened once or twice – I've been able to vector down to a less terrifying altitude without flapping, when panicking might have caused a terrible accident. On three separate occasions I've saved a person's life, one of them after they'd choked at the dinner table, thumping them on the back until the piece of food was dislodged from their windpipe. In stressful circumstances, then, I've been able to function effectively and my experiences in the military had toughened me, preparing my psyche for a second career of creative adversity. Mentally, I was ready for anything.

A t night, I ran.

Not the sort of evening jog as enjoyed by most runners in order to shake away the day's frustrations, but through the early hours. Often I'd wake at two or three in the morning, unable to sleep, the thought of whatever challenge was facing me at BP tweaking my brain. Rather than lie awake in a fitful state, I'd pull on my trainers and get some fresh air, my mind slowly drawing together ideas, plans and conclusions. This is a habit that can benefit us all. Scientists have found that running quickly for thirty minutes improves our 'cortical flicker threshold', which allows us to process information more clearly. It also improves executive function, which means we can focus and problem-solve more easily – though doctor's orders would probably recommend you run during the day rather than in the middle of the night.

As a kid I used to find running very difficult; I really wouldn't have been considered a natural runner by any of my PE teachers while at Queen's College. I abhorred cross-country running because that was a mandatory physical activity at school: I wasn't one for being told what to do. It also seemed such an unpleasant experience. Who genuinely enjoyed getting freezing cold, wet and muddy while their lungs burned and their hamstrings twanged? However, fast-forward twenty years and, given how it's been a physical outlet for emotional pain, I can honestly say, 'Yes, I do love running.' As I've grown older, I've realized that stretching my legs in such a way is the only thing that calms what has become a very overactive mind. With my feet pounding the pavement, or countryside, I'm able to problem-solve; I make connections to issues and ideas at the forefront of my brain, and have even enjoyed several Eureka! moments on the road. I'm able to settle into an inner calmness that I'd ordinarily struggle to locate solely by slouching on the sofa, and these days I rarely run less than 10 or 15 kilometres whenever I decide to take a leisurely jog.

Typically, in May 2016, I went to the extremes in exploring my love of physical exercise when I took on my first ultra-marathon. As the name might suggest, the concept of such a race is to run a marathon-style event and then run it again, and again. It's just about as hardcore as long-distance running gets. Its definition stands as 'any footrace longer than the traditional marathon length of 42 kilometres, or 26 miles', but sometimes they can last for many hundreds of miles.

I chose to do my first one because I wanted to push myself really hard, but what I soon came to appreciate, apart from the enduring hardship that would rack my body for most of the race, was the deep exploration of the inner workings of the mind that took place while running alone, often in silence, for hours and hours on end (over demanding terrain, these races could last for longer than twenty-four hours). There were moments of ecstasy, flashes of fear; minutes where taking the next step seemed almost impossible; periods of time when the pace and effort arrived easily. But through all those emotions and sensations, the mind always worked alone, unencumbered by distractions, apart from the Zen-like motion of placing one foot in front of the other and the sound of rubber striking the ground below.

I wouldn't recommend signing up to an ultra-marathon in haste. It's very much something that needs to be worked up to slowly, and with care. The longest race I have ever taken part in was the famous Ridgeway Challenge, an 86-mile-long trial that begins at the Ivinghoe Beacon near Tring in Hertfordshire before winding over a track reported to be 5,000 years old, which at one point crosses the charmingly titled Grim's Ditch in the North Wessex Downs. It's here that the finishing line finally, blessedly, comes into sight at the Avebury Stone Circle. As you can imagine, my experience of the race was painful, rewarding and a little weird. The running began on a Saturday morning, with the competitors moving throughout the day and night, though at one juncture there was a checkpoint at which we stopped briefly to grab a serving of hot food and change our sodden socks in a dry area.

Having made it so far, I was feeling strong and fairly confident of finishing in good time. But then, as I wolfed down a bowl of soup, a somewhat unhelpful volunteer forgot it had been his job to support the knackered runners queuing up for sustenance.

'Good luck everybody,' he shouted. 'The night stage is where most competitors drop out.'

My body and soul were a little dampened by that.

It had been a gloomy evening, accompanied by a mist of drizzly rain, but psychologically the Ridgeway Challenge instantly became a much sterner test. Guided by the narrow pool of light projecting from my headlamp on to the terrain below – which comprised a white chalk pathway no more than 8 inches in width – I ran over uneven ground for around five more hours, into the early morning. With hindsight I could think of a few better ways to mentally torture oneself. I'd been on the move for around eighteen hours and my resolve was being tested again. All bodily reserves had been depleted. My temperature regulation had gone screwy and one minute I shivered with cold, the next I was sweating profusely and overheating. Essentially my body was very low on calorific reserves. Despite my efforts to take in food, you can't consume as fast as you metabolize on the move. You can almost feel your body hunting around for ways to save energy. Meanwhile, an inner voice kept whispering, 'Richard, do you really want to keep on doing this? You know, you could just quit.'

I held firm, shushing the inner couch potato, but near the finishing line, with my arduous task almost complete, I took yet another funny turn. According to historians, the Avebury stone circles were built and then shaped throughout the Neolithic period, when a group of intrepid workmen constructed an impressive ring that now encompasses the village of Avebury. As the sun emerged over the horizon and burned away the morning mist, I glimpsed their majesty: a series of huge impressive stones were spread across the rolling fields, but to my mind the nearest one was definitely an elephant, complete with a trunk, tusks and four legs. I saw it vividly ahead of me. I *knew* it wasn't really an elephant. I *knew* I was hallucinating. And yet there it was, its wrinkled shape squatting quietly in the near distance. My brain had become so tired and low on energy that even the basic function of identifying an image captured by my retinas had failed. Upon reflection, it was a fascinating moment, an interesting way of accessing what is an unusual trippy failure within the recesses of the mind. But, bloody hell, was it hard work getting there. And I wouldn't recommend the required workload to anyone.

Workshop Notes

THINK LIKE A SOLDIER TO INNOVATE

The military teaches us about perseverance. There's a belief that every step forward is progress, no matter how small. If we can drag ourselves one more inch through the mud, well, that's success.

There are parallels between the culture of start-ups and the process of innovation. By definition we're going out on a limb, doing something nobody else has done successfully before. We don't know if we're going to make it but we've got to convince ourselves that we can. When our motivation seems to be running out of steam, or when we've been so ground down by criticism and setbacks that pushing on seems too difficult, remember . . . *we can go beyond.*

Takeaways

○ Learning to operate like a soldier can help us find the perseverance to see tricky business plans through to the end, or to make it through some of the more gruelling processes of innovation. We might think we can't make it to the end and there will be a growing pressure to quit at times; we might get bogged down in heavy workloads or become ambushed by sticky situations. We should always remember that simply to put one foot in front of the other is progress, just as they do in the military.

○ Recognize exercise as a workspace. It's possible to creatively problem-solve and generate truly insightful ideas during the escape of physical training.

TRADING PLACES

Or, Why Ignoring Conventional Wisdom and
Embracing Change Can Be a Good Idea

et me tell you the story about Kodak.

In 1975 the globally famous camera company invented digital photography. Plans to release this new technology into the market were considered, and one or two link-up projects with software firms were even discussed, but Kodak's expansion was eventually shelved. The general concern among the company's leading thinkers was that nobody was going to get excited about computerized pictures. It was a fad, a flash-in-the-pan idea.

But they were wrong.

At first, the idea that digital technology might change how the world used photography had seemed distant and unlikely. The company later introduced digital photography into their output, but it was too late. Kodak eventually lost their market share as a raft of disruptive industries such as smartphones and picture apps were made affordable and accessible. By failing to capitalize on an opportunity that went on to be grasped by other tech companies, Kodak misread the true point of their business. They believed they'd understood their customers, and what their customers wanted was tangible memories: photographs that could be held, shared, and placed into frames or albums. From a consumer's point of view, however, a disruptive and forward-thinking technology had popped up that allowed them to capture, store and share those memories more effectively. Kodak fell away.

There are plenty of examples of companies that have failed to steer a new course or adapt, having spotted an iceberg on the horizon. Of course, it's very hard to predict the emergence of these issues – none of us has a crystal ball at our disposal – yet having encountered one, the affected should deploy the open-mindedness and innovative spirit needed to ask difficult questions, such as, 'Hang on, are we thinking about our business in the wrong way?' Instead, Kodak became stuck in the groove of what they were currently doing, losing sight of where their real value was and how to adapt to changing times. This is not a new phenomenon either. Before the motorcar, hay distribution was a thriving industry in cities such as New York and London. Hay fed the horses that pulled the carts; the carts transported passengers and goods over long distances. In essence it was fuel before petrol or diesel. But did farmers and hay salesmen pivot to petrol when it was hinted that the motorcar might take over the world? Sadly not. Hay companies went bust in large numbers, their owners too slow and set in their ways to realize that nobody would want to buy hay any more because the world was about to undergo a fundamental change. Different suppliers emerged to provide a new fuel for this new form of popular transport.

Around 2012 I looked at the oil industry and suspected a similar situation.

Huge companies like BP are vulnerable to a range of disruptive factors. At BP, some of them were self-inflicted, such as the 2010 *Deepwater Horizon* catastrophe: an explosion on an offshore drilling rig and the resulting leak spilled 210 million US gallons into the Gulf of Mexico, an environmental disaster that led to calls for tighter regulations and an increase in more environmentally acceptable energy resources. Those resources themselves had to be considered as challenges to the industry's established players too. Solar and wind energy were becoming popular, as well as more affordable. Meanwhile, the price of oil was often volatile and expensive, and wars and geopolitics were having a major impact on supply and therefore cost. Once again the world was changing, and perhaps that presented an opportunity.

I looked at the historical examples of Kodak and others and realized that BP wasn't rooted in the business of selling oil. In reality, the company traded in heat, light and mobility, and there were a number of alternative technologies emerging that we needed to explore in order to progress, especially given the huge assets and momentum at

161

our fingertips. For example, renewable energy, or more environmentally friendly extraction methods, were affordable to us, as were many other new technologies. But, like many people, I understood that encouraging a company as big and sometimes unwieldy as BP to embrace any form of disruptive technology in one fell swoop was a tall order. For true and lasting change to be implemented, several small but significant tweaks would have to be made to the way the industry worked, and all the while senior management figures would have to be emboldened to explore the benefit of new technologies. And not just in the way the company sold energy, but in its working practices too.

I was about to swim against the tide once more.

Workshop Notes

LOOK FOR THE ICEBERGS

An increasing number of businesses go under having ignored disruptive rivals exploring a better, upgraded product. The traditional taxi trade suffered because of the emergence of Uber and several other ride-sharing apps. The music industry struggled to maintain its late twentieth-century profit margins thanks to cut-price streaming services such as Spotify. And national newspapers, once a mainstay of commuting culture and weekend reading, have been left fighting for survival as online media has become easily accessible on laptops and smartphones. There's an argument that all of these industries could have thrived had they noticed the icebergs looming on the horizon earlier, and adapted accordingly.

The best way to spot these icebergs is to be inquisitive, while taking small risks to explore emerging markets and ideas. An airline, for example, might want to look into hyperloops, the technology being championed by Elon Musk that could enable us to travel around the world at record speeds. Instead of sitting in a boardroom dismissing the idea as something beyond our grasp, why not invest a small amount in one of the companies experimenting in the field? It's important to retain the childlike inquisitiveness that repeatedly asks 'Why not?' and 'What if?'.

When a threat looms, it's unwise to ignore it. Instead, we should explore any advances in technology and what they might mean for our business; we need to understand how any innovations in our industry might upgrade the work we do. Only then can we avoid nasty collisions in the future.

n 2012, my first step was to look at blockchain. Within BP much had already been said about the technology, which is a computer code platform that allows for secure transactions and exchanges of information that can be decentralized, so there isn't a single server or point of potential failure. Crypto-currencies such as Bitcoin used blockchain to record transactions. Elsewhere, banks and financial institutions were taking on digital distributed ledgers to share data globally. There was a feeling that blockchain might revolutionize the way everybody conducted their business and a number of studies were commissioned by BP to assess its potential. People were getting very excited and holding all kinds of meetings, but a real-world sense of what could be achieved by using blockchain didn't exist. Everything was theoretical.

The challenge I took upon myself was to turn theory into practicality.

The kind of transactions into which blockchain was being implemented were the kind that regularly took place at BP. Within the energy industry, many people had oil to sell but not all of them were trustworthy. As a result, global companies such as BP often had departments that ran character checks on the groups they traded with. It was a common-sense policy that ensured we didn't hand over millions of pounds to somebody who might turn out to be a covert arms dealer or militia group leader. Known as the Trading Accounts Opening Team, it was this group's frankly pain-in-the-arse task to verify and background-check everybody hoping to exchange with BP. To my thinking it made sense to create a Shared Ledger of Trust – a system where everybody shared intelligence on their trading partners. But because of the nature of energy trading, where marginal gains translated into millions of pounds, nobody wanted to give away too much information about who was trading with whom. Still, such a system might save time and resources when digging into the hopefully-not-murky backstory of any new clients. And this was exactly the sort of resource that blockchain was designed for.

In the years since GEM's introduction, my new position as a technologist had given me a level of freedom in which to explore new innovations, as long as they were linked to the energy industry. Enthused by the potential of marrying a Shared Ledger of Trust – a process that everybody viewed as being a necessary evil – to an exciting new digital system, I hired two PhD graduates capable of writing a blockchain app in one afternoon. I linked them to the Trading Accounts Opening Team and suddenly the system was ahead of us – a set-up that enabled the company to share background information with a list of energy firms without exposing any secrets or highly sensitive details to those same firms. The whole process cost a few thousand quid. Even better, BP was now able to see that blockchain had real benefits for the industry and beyond.

Having demystified one fast-moving strand of new tech, I felt the urge to do more, exploring all kinds of software and science. I eventually returned to the concept of shipping safety, where I'd learned that the vast majority of accidents were being caused by fatigue. Captains on tankers often worked through eighteen-hour shifts, sometimes in treacherous and stormy conditions. Relatively simple tasks such as steering through an obstacle course of tiny barges moored in Rotterdam harbour became incredibly hazardous due to a lack of sleep. In 2011, Cardiff University had even conducted studies that compared fatigue to alcohol consumption: it was discovered that four-and-a-half hours spent behind the wheel was similar to being over the legal alcohol limit in a car. When it came to oil shipping, mistakes – big or small – tended to be expensive.

'Hmm,' I thought. 'I bet there's another industry that's dealt with issues of sleep deprivation . . . *How about truck driving?*'

I called around, and discovered that the road transport industry had indeed reappraised its attitudes to fatigue, which was understandable given that there were a number of unpleasant risks associated with falling asleep at the wheel. What was interesting was that a number of haulage companies had solved this particular issue with the help of different technologies, one of which was a wearable gadget, the kind made popular by companies such as Fitbit. Apparently, this technology was very good at detecting basic parameters, such as the number of miles walked and heart rate, but with one or two upgrades a similar device affixed to the dashboard of a truck was now capable of analysing eyeball movement. From its readings, a computer decided whether or not the driver was fit to push on down the motorway. If he or she had become too fatigued, an alert flashed on the system that instructed them to pull over at the nearest motorway service station – presumably to nap, or load up on caffeine.

I sourced the name of a company that specialized in this form of tech. At first they seemed oblivious to the potential of shifting their operations from the M25 into the North Sea, but having explained, approximately, just how many ships and ship operators were involved on a daily basis, their interest spiked. The numbers were huge, as was the potential for a handsome profit, and they delivered a set of wearable equipment that BP was able to test during an experimental phase. Within a month our prototypes were so successful they'd been widely implemented across the entire fleet.

There were upswings and downswings to executing these projects, as I discovered to my cost. The upswings were that I'd validated a quite sensible approach of twinning internal domain experts, such as the Trading Accounts Opening Team, with an external, creative concept such as blockchain. The fact that exploratory missions of this kind improved the company's working practices and tended to be quite cheap only added to their appeal. Or so I thought. The dramatic downswing was that in the process I'd ruffled a few feathers among the senior management team, who were already pissed off that a large number of the trading staff were earning considerably larger salaries than they were, despite being much younger. I was soon viewed as a relatively junior and cheeky staff member with a gadget fetish. The fact that my new ideas seemed to be pushing BP into a forward-thinking and, in their opinion, unpredictable direction had only upset them further. My superiors were of the opposite mind-set to me. Change, they argued, was *a very bad thing*.

Shortly after my successful work with the anti-fatigue system I was called into a management meeting where I expected to be rewarded with a pat on the back. Instead I was rounded upon in a corporate ambush. I won't mention names, or job titles, but I was told to listen closely, for my 'own benefit', as the ringleader of this group loomed over his desk and issued a stark warning.

'You're way out of your depth, Richard,' he snarled. 'What you're doing isn't welcomed.'

I was taken aback. Surely I was saving the company millions? And what was the harm in helping to ease the workload of the Trading Accounts Opening Team, or stopping ship captains from ploughing into tiny barges docked in Rotterdam harbour?

My oppressor was having none of it.

'Innovation is a mechanism by which you introduce risk into a business,' he said.

Now I was confused. Yes, innovation could be considered as such. But conversely, it might also be considered as the best mechanism for delivering reward into a business. Were all of us to apply the same logic to life, it's unlikely anybody would leave the house for fear of something going wrong. Taking risks is the best way of ensuring progress; all of us benefit from new ideas. Also, my understanding was that I worked in an industry where dreaming outside the box was essential. If an oil trader wasn't creatively scheming a huge deal, or seeking an edge over the competition, they were unlikely to last too long in the game. This was a job that thrived on calculated gambles.

What I'd failed to grasp was that a culture of fear had gripped the company in the wake of the *Deepwater Horizon* scandal. Within senior circles, a large number of individuals had become fearful of change; they wanted to stabilize any unpredictable moving parts in the company's practices. As a result I'd become regarded as a loose cannon. With hindsight, it was all very tragic. Carrying a risk-averse worldview made navigating what became a decade of revolution in energy supply a little trickier. Like those haymakers in the early twentieth century, when motorcars began to revolutionize travel and fuel consumption, BP had forgotten they were in the business of heat, light and mobility rather than oil. But if they improved those three strands of their business by alternative, forward-thinking means with speed, their longevity was ensured.

Not everybody in the room thought that way.

'There are people with big boots around you and they're not afraid to use them,' I was told ominously.

There was no doubt in my mind that the senior management team had hoped to back me into a corner, and I was a little shaken for sure. Threatened by the serious consequences of what might happen should I fail to comply with their requests, I thanked them all for their advice and left the room.

Then I returned to my desk and carried on just as before.

Workshop Notes

DON'T ALWAYS LISTEN TO THE GROWN-UPS IN THE ROOM

The desire to dismiss expert opinion has become very fashionable in the era of Trump and Brexit, but I don't subscribe to that entirely. Still, I admit that when senior figures at established institutions become focused on maintaining the status quo, it becomes very hard for them to birth ideas that might challenge their learned behaviour. They play it safe and seek to repeat what has worked in the past. Sadly, this situation is the very enemy of innovation: nobody wants to move forward for fear of making a mistake.

It's not like that everywhere, however. Institutions such as NASA can be credited with examples of having their thinking challenged by people who might not necessarily be considered experts. In a programme called NASA Solve, they often throw a tricky issue out to the public, hoping somebody, somewhere, might have an idea they haven't previously considered. NASA has realized the importance of humility and left-field thought when pushing for innovation. The results have been wonderfully refreshing.

Elsewhere, the toy company LEGO have allowed customers to submit their ideas for new play sets. A voting system was set up and any ideas that received 10,000 or more approvals from customers were then put into production. The person behind the idea was then invited to help with its development, later receiving royalty payments upon its release.

> I've used outsider ideas when working on the jet
> suit. Quite recently I received an email from somebody
> working on the production line at an airbag factory. He
> wondered if the same technology could be implemented
> into the jet suit and sent a note suggesting as much. It
> wasn't long before we agreed he could be on to something
> and prototyped the idea.
>
> Expert thinking should always be considered, but
> sometimes it helps to listen to the outsiders with a
> different perspective.

n business, as in life, we experience good and bad luck. The trick is to make the most of good fortune when it shines on us. And when my moment came at work, I'd squeezed it for everything I could.

From the mid-2000s I worked for BP with one goal in mind: I wanted to buy myself a sense of freedom – and I was on the right path to do so, having passed my 'assessed traders' entry course in 2004 in quite an unusual manner. A week-long residential programme, the examination requires candidates to pretty much live in a hotel with a trading screen positioned in the bedroom, in what was considered a death-or-glory assessment. The stakes were incredibly high. Pass and I'd be ushered into the hallowed halls of market trading with the potential to rake in a lot of money; fail and I'd be consigned to the comparatively humble role of an analyst, or operator, with my tail between my legs. I'd heard plenty of stories of wannabe traders walking around the building with the 'Big I Am' attitude in the weeks building up to their trading course. Having been crushed during the assessments, they'd returned to their former posts in a state of embarrassment. Emotionally it was a gruelling and humbling experience, and a number of failing attendees quit shortly afterwards, knowing they had been cut off at the knees, unable to progress towards their goal.

I was sponsored to take the trading course thanks in no small part to my work on the GEM project, although in the months leading up to it I had effectively been working as a very junior trader, even though I hadn't passed the requisite tests at that time. Having developed GEM, I'd blended my role as a technologist with a position on the crude oil team, which was a gateway route into serious trading, where the big bucks were made. But rather than follow a set path to bigger, more lucrative commodities, I ventured towards something brand new and untried at the time: petrochemicals.

The petrochemical market was a fresh venture for BP, and I was in there like a shot, travelling to new territories and carving out unusual trading opportunities. Given that many of the countries – Mozambique, Turkmenistan, Libya – were pretty much off the grid in tourism terms, my day-to-day work took on a higher level of personal risk, and I revelled in it.

My back-to-front enrolment wasn't anything out of the ordinary. Compared to most people at the company, I was known for operating in a left-field style. Once the course had started, I held my own, fancying my chances in the final test – the mother of all personal examinations in which everybody traded multiple oil grades, ran refineries and analysed shipments on a simulator amid overloaded circumstances designed to apply impossible pressure. Except, I wouldn't know because I didn't make it that far.

For the past twenty-four hours I'd been experiencing intermittent stabbing pains in my lower abdomen. I often forgot about it during the day because I was so busy, but in those brief lulls between simulations it would flare up, until I couldn't ignore it any longer. Over dinner the possibility of appendicitis was suggested, so I walked to the local Accident and Emergency, where I waited for several hours as a series of more critical patients came and went. When my turn arrived, I was subjected to a series of undignified tests, my career as a trader hanging in the balance. The golden rule of the BP trading entry course was there were no second chances. Everybody got one shot, and one shot only.

'This is the worst possible preparation for a life-changing day,' I thought as a doctor pushed his finger into a very intimate part of my anatomy. Things were soon to get worse.

'Mr Browning, you're not going anywhere,' the doctor said as he yanked off his rubber gloves with a snap. 'Your appendix is in a critical state. It could burst at any moment. We're going to have to whip it out immediately.'

My days of trading glory were a fading dream.

'But . . . I've got a trading course to do. My final exam is tomorrow!'

The doctor was unimpressed at my dilemma and moments later I left a very sheepish voicemail for the course leader, knowing it was highly unlikely I'd have another chance at passing the test. 'They're about to take my appendix out,' I moaned. 'I'm really sorry. I'll be unconscious by the time you get this message. I don't know what to say . . .'

Matters weren't helped by the fact I'd already committed a cardinal sin in trading terms. Just hours previously, during a particularly stressful moment in the simulations, I had failed to vet a ship for its approval status within the stringent BP systems. It was very much considered a black mark – not quite a knockout blow to my hopes, but a downer all the same. I was due to be hauled over the coals about it the following day, and even though I had confidence that the work I'd done up to that point was enough to stand me in good stead for the final assessments, I still had to end the course well – really well. Now, instead, I was going under a general anaesthetic.

I tried to be philosophical about the turn of events. I told myself that the route fate had set for me was out of my hands. As I drifted away – a surgeon looming over me – my mind was set: I was joining a long line of crushed hopefuls; when I awoke my appendix would be in a bin somewhere, along with my trading career.

And that's when my lucky break arrived.

When I came to, a savage scar lined across my belly, my wife frantically calling the hospital to find out how I was, word was delivered from BP. Apparently they were going to pass me, just, regardless of my blunder on the penultimate day. A strong track record within the company and my work up until that point had indeed stood me in good stead. I was deemed worthy of a place on BP's trading-room floor, my legend assured as the only trader to have passed the infamous entry course without completing the exam, though it had taken a near-death experience to secure me that status. As I prepared for my prestigious new role in the company, I was determined to make the most of my opportunity.

knuckled down and eschewed the trappings of those yearly BP bonuses (bar the occasional five-quid watch from Amazon, of course). Instead I saved, knowing deep down that the job was my route to the financial security I craved, even if the culture wasn't really me. Even the people who understood me better than anyone, like my mother, sensed a life in the City was at odds with my personality.

'I'm really surprised you're a trader,' she'd say, time after time. 'It's not something I thought you would do.'

I often shrugged my shoulders and batted away the statement, though she was right. Deep down I'd always craved to be different. I needed to be creative. I wanted to innovate more freely and on my own terms, alone, without supervision. But there was a hitch. I was scared of taking the first step into an independent world where there was a lack of financial and professional security, especially with a series of domestic commitments hanging over my head, such as our growing family and our home. I couldn't face a repeat of my childhood experiences. I didn't want a career gamble to impinge on the lives of my family, and the emotional pressures that came with that.

Part of my anxiety towards monetary risk was attributable to the tragedies of my father's life. I certainly have a disproportionate nervousness regarding financial hardship – real or imagined – even though I knew my role in one of the biggest trading hubs in the world put me in a secure position. The very idea that I might be heading down a pathway of financial discomfort was enough to fill me with a deep and irrational sense of dread – it still is. It's so bad that even the mention of a business plan or start-up idea from a friend is enough to send me off on one about the dangers of giving up the day job to pursue their venture. To some people their ideas might sound like a worthwhile risk. To my mind it sets off all sorts of alarm bells. That sense of déjà vu was brought on entirely by my father's choices and the unravelling of his life as a consequence.

So to prepare the ground for a life of creative freedom, I strived to pay off the mortgage as quickly as I could. We'd moved into a bigger house in Salisbury, where I had the space to work on crazy garden projects for the kids and build a workshop for myself in which I tinkered and planned at the weekends. I didn't know what I wanted to do beyond working for BP just yet, but it was something other than the conventional route – commuting into London for the next twenty years. A change was needed, if I was to be truly happy.

I worked and saved, giving myself the wriggle room to imagine a time when I could innovate freely at home without worrying about pay cheques and bank balances. I was also weirdly inspired by some of the setbacks I'd experienced while working on projects as a technologist, where I'd found incentive in people's negative reactions. I realized that if it wasn't pushing against the tide, I wasn't interested, and it was that mood of unruliness that took me to my next adventure – my best design yet.

I had decided to build a flying machine.

Workshop Notes

DREAM ON A BUDGET

I once heard an interview with the former Formula One Group chief executive Bernie Ecclestone. In it, he argued that his sole ambition had never been to earn huge amounts of money (though he admitted it had become a nice bellweather of success). Instead, he'd wanted to follow his dreams. This description of his ambitions was quite eloquently put, I thought. I realized that if somebody was forever chasing cash, it's unlikely they'd experience the same heartfelt drive as another person doing a job for love, something they'd have involved themselves in for free.

When deciding what I wanted to do next, I required that same sense of motivation. I needed to earn the money up front, rather than chasing it later.

Thankfully at BP I was in a position to build a healthy financial safety net for myself, and also found a balance that allowed me to innovate in my own time. I know that isn't the case for everybody. Still, we can all follow a similar set of rules. When looking to begin a new business, whether as a start-up or simply when working on an innovative idea, it's imperative we assess the financial risks at all times because operating with a financial gun to the head can be unpleasant. Quite simply, if the investment of both time and money requires you to risk significant hardship then you and your family need to be fully prepared for that.

Takeaways

○ Look to the disruptive industries, companies, business leaders and innovations in your field for inspiration. What can we learn from them?

○ Beware the institutionalized experts. Senior figures sometimes err on the side of caution, which is the enemy of innovation.

○ Prepare a financial safety net before making a life-changing leap into a new project. Sleepless nights spent worrying about paying the bills can wreck the creative process.

11

IT *IS* ROCKET SCIENCE

Or, How Science Fiction, Famous Innovators and the Military Elite Inspired Me to Start a Business

By late 2016 I had a functioning jet suit – a product that worked, and something I felt deserved to be launched properly and shared with the world. But this would have to be done with a lot of thought and care, because something so new, so unknown, could land with the media and public in any number of ways, not all of them positive.

As a start-up founder or innovator, or even a small-business owner, it's vital to consider the brand you are building. When I first committed to launching the company which came to be Gravity Industries, I knew I'd have to build a strong brand from scratch, and quickly, too. I was forever hearing that new businesses had to create a powerful identity because anyone could copy a great idea, but it is so much harder to copy a company's entire identity. This was reassuring to learn. When I started the company I had three very distinct values in mind, which featured a blend of fictional mavericks, fearless inventors and military trailblazers that I hoped would represent the ethos and aspirations of my endeavour.

The fictional maverick I had in mind was Tony Stark, or Iron Man, and his Hollywood character was apt and inspiring in a number of ways. Apt because in one scene the inventor tests his flying suit in a lab, crashing into a line-up of parked cars and hi-tech equipment at speed, which was a slightly upmarket portrayal of my early R&D flights once I'd started work. He also balances in mid-air in the same way I do in flight, though I really should have paid closer attention to those painful collisions in his testing phases – it might have spared me from some of the bumps and bruises that followed. Nevertheless, his character was an inspiring identity for the company. Stark, and likewise Bruce Wayne of Batman fame, were successful individuals in their own right, working in the real commercial world during business hours. I loved the idea that both characters were achievers in a conventional way, but in their spare time explored ideas and built concepts in their man caves before doing something exceptional with their work. The duopoly of roles – average bloke and, in their case, superhero – was incredibly appealing.

I'm no superhero, though there are undeniably one or two similarities in our respective origin stories. There was also the moral dilemma of how my technology might be used in the future. But that was never a focus when I constructed the suit; simply getting off the ground was my only ambition.

Inspiration number two for Gravity Industries' DNA was the twenty-first century's raft of radical business thinkers, which included the likes of Elon Musk (Tesla), Steve Jobs (Apple), Sheryl Sandberg and Mark Zuckerberg (Facebook) – people unafraid to think outside the parameters of what was traditionally considered possible; individuals who weren't afraid to fail in the pursuit of their ambitions. When I first set out to design a jet suit, most people weren't convinced it was achievable; the idea it might be produced as a viable consumer product was dismissed out of hand. But I didn't allow the doubters to dissuade me. I often thought back to the work of Sir Richard Branson and the failures he endured before finding success, particularly during his attempts to break world records around the globe. Branson had appealed to me as a kid because of his intrepid spirit. He inspired me later on in life because he was never upended by the bumps on his road to success.

In 1968, *Student* magazine was Branson's first business venture, but income quickly became a problem so he changed path and launched a mail-order record company that later evolved into the multi-billion-dollar label Virgin Records. There are other tales of against-the-odds adventures. When in 1991 his Pacific hot-air balloon flight began to lose fuel and careered towards the water, his chances of survival seemed grim. Rather than give up and resign himself to certain death among the huge waves whipped up by gale-force winds, Branson and his co-pilot stayed up for three days without sleep in an attempt to reach the coast.

'Never give up,' he said afterwards. 'Even if it sounds slightly corny. Fight, fight, fight to survive.'

It's worth remembering that Virgin Atlantic, his hugely successful transatlantic airline, very nearly failed to get off the ground in 1984 when a bird strike grounded his only plane during a test flight. A Civil Aviation Authority assessor had sat next to Branson during the ill-fated take-off, but Virgin passed all the other tests and once a new engine had been secured, the company was granted a licence. The business went from strength to strength.

The third and final strand of the Gravity Industries DNA was the example set by the British Special Forces, the elite unit of the military that operates from the shadows in some of the world's most danger-ous war zones. I loved the mystery of their work, shot through with adrenalin and a real sense of purpose, and I subscribed to the idea that people were able to push themselves to their absolute physical and mental limits to get the job done.

The military taught me a great deal about how best to handle the stresses associated with working on a new idea that others consider odd-ball, or frivolous. But to my mind special ops work and innovation are linked even more explicitly. Both working practices carry a sense of autonomy, requiring people to think on their feet in challenging situ-ations rather than simply take orders. Both need to be fearless, too. When an innovator or soldier glimpses that ominous signpost at the beginning of an adventure marked 'It's Impossible: Do Not Enter', they don't shy away. They wrench the signpost from the ground and walk in anyway.

Endurance athletes act in pretty much the same way. Whether it's in business or extreme sports, there is a shared spirit of defiance, a desire to break boundaries, and within each person the desire to go further than they've ever been before. The achievement aspect of that attitude is incredibly addictive. Once an innovator has struck his first investment deal for a new project, the feeling isn't one of smug satisfaction. There is no time to reflect or to self-indulge. Instead the focus switches to the next test, the next obstacle. For the newly appointed Special Forces operator it might be that first taste of elite action; the start-up visionary, energized by funding, is inspired to seek out more exposure and investment. There are always more questions to answer. *What else can I achieve? What might I do next?*

Finding the answers becomes compulsive.

My mind had been set on inventing a new method of flight, and from my homemade workshop I designed and built throughout 2016 in my spare time. Many, many prototypes came and went. Strange parcels frequently arrived from Amazon or eBay containing items I'd planned to repurpose into a functional jet suit system, including those baby carriers which were turned into an exoskeleton of sorts: a fuel tank had to be strapped to my back and the toddler harness was ideally suited to hold it in place. For several months I ran on fumes as I worked into the night, every night, figuring out how to overcome various problems, until eventually I possessed a fully functioning flying machine that I knew, in theory, was capable of taking me into the air for several minutes. My workshop was a jumble of turbine parts, jet fuel bags and weird half-built structures.

As I advanced, my curious little secret was suddenly a subtle conversation starter. I wasn't openly bragging about my small victories in the workshop to BP's team of traders, or expanding a social media profile. Instead I'd decided to keep my achievements under the radar for a while. I believed in what I was doing, for sure; I'd become confident the work could inspire people and maybe change the way society thought about flight, which was everything for me at that point. But I wanted to reveal whatever this jet suit might become with a clear and considered narrative. Luckily, the ways and means of doing so were very close to home.

I'd found myself moving within an interesting network of technology entrepreneurs, thanks to my rogue technologist activity at BP. Every now and then I'd take a meeting with an innovator or creative from a certain field, often pulling out my phone before we parted.

'By the way, you'll never guess what I was doing at the weekend,' I'd say, watching their reactions with interest as I proudly played a grainy video of the six-second flight I had achieved in the farmer's yard.

The clip elicited an identical response whenever I played it. *What the hell's that? That's super-cool!* I suppose I was polling for an opinion, in one sense; and any enthusiasm for my extra-curricular work from big-city technologists validated my gut feeling that I had embarked on a worthwhile adventure. Meanwhile, every viewing expanded my contacts base. Whenever I showed the footage, the details of someone who might have a serious interest in what I was doing arrived in my email inbox shortly afterwards.

One of these characters was an investor named Anthony Ganjou, a friend of a friend who had made good money from a number of interesting business ventures. One of these was sky-typing, a concept in which a small fleet of planes fly around in formation, puffing out coloured smoke in such a way that their trails spell out a word or symbol. He was also behind the innovative concept of clean graffiti. This was another creative marketing tool in which graffiti was stencilled on to a wall, or other surface, but because the inks were made of a substance that rendered them temporary it was possible to wash away an advert or mural with a power hose. Anthony was known for building the foundations of his businesses on clear branding and eye-catching PR mechanisms. He was exactly the type of person I'd hoped might take an interest in my jet suit prototype and offer me some feedback.

At the end of 2016 we were introduced on email, and we met up at Waterloo Station one day during rush hour. Anthony arrived looking rather smart; I was somewhat more down at heel, kitted head to foot in cycling Lycra, as I prepared to make the long commute home.

Immediately he struck me as a quirky guy. Anthony was deadpan, the sort of person who might do very well in a game of poker. For our entire conversation, his facial expressions gave nothing away. In fact I'd go so far as to say he looked pretty pissed off as I showed him the video. He nodded and mumbled some vaguely positive but noncommittal congratulations and then we boarded our respective trains home. I spent the journey feeling somewhat underwhelmed by the encounter, and filed away our meeting as a nice but ultimately fruitless endeavour. I didn't expect to hear from him again.

But I did, in January 2017. God knows what happened in the interim period, but something must have stoked Anthony's fire because he came barrelling back into the conversation as if the life of his family depended upon it. There were emails full of determination. I was left totally bemused by his newfound energy. At that stage he hadn't seen a real-life demo. In fact, outside of my family and close friends, nobody had. But after one or two conversations we agreed to meet again in London, where Anthony made a staggering offer.

'I'm up for investing £100,000,' he said. 'Not only do I think this is cool, even without properly seeing it, but with my PR, marketing, media, attention-grabbing hat on, I think there's something really powerful in this. I'm willing to believe in you.'

I was amazed, flattered, and somewhat caught off guard. I hadn't even thought of starting up a company, let alone seeking out investors. It was as if a passing asteroid had nudged my happily orbiting satellite away from BP's gravitational pull. I was spun into a new trajectory, one that required fresh ideas, different ways of thinking, creative procedures. That independent and informed vote of confidence had a profound effect, for which I'm very grateful.

'Holy shit,' I thought. 'Against all of my instincts, and fears, I really am going to step away from this lucrative, comfortable, long-term money-paying future and believe in myself. If Anthony is willing to put £100,000 in, then I will set myself on this path.'

Life had handed me a new set of coordinates.

A nthony changed the game.

He helped to create a name for my work-in-progress company: Gravity, though a few alternatives were cut away in the meantime. Of these, one was Thrust, which carried a number of dodgy connotations, as you can imagine, so when Anthony later suggested Gravity Industries as a front-of-house moniker, the title landed: the name described exactly the sandbox I'd been playing in, while delivering a sense of exploration and aeronautical adventure. Even better, the title hadn't been trademarked in the arena of aeronautics, so we pressed ahead with establishing what was then a small workshop outfit. The time had come to launch a start-up venture that would hopefully gain an innovative, slightly eccentric but hopefully entertaining and inspiring reputation around the world.

I was keenly aware that first impressions were everything in technology, especially where the British media were concerned. The tabloid press loved nothing more than to mock an eccentric inventor, somebody designing elaborate and messy constructions from their backwater garage in the style of the early twentieth-century maverick William Heath Robinson, a creator who became synonymous with building ludicrously complex designs for machines that performed basic tasks. I also understood my performance was key, and the thought of being portrayed as a slightly delusional boffin filled me with dread. The last thing I wanted was to arrive at a launch event in a space-age jet suit and futuristic crash helmet, my engines spluttering to failure as I stood rooted on terra firma. My first public appearance had to be inspiring. Most of all, it had to be cool.

Which was where *Wired* and Red Bull came in.

Wired is a magazine that brims with stories of nerdy but very cool innovation – a ballpark where my work might fit quite nicely. Red Bull were an equally exciting platform but in a very different reaction. The energy drinks brand-turned-adrenalin sports behemoth had long been a disruptive figure in the extreme-sports arena. Having dominated YouTube with their videos of mountain bikers, wingsuit

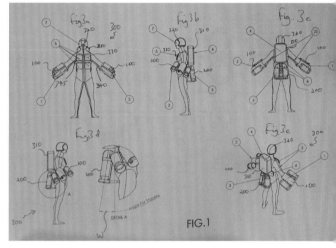

Top: A busy garage workshop, in the days before we were able to build a custom facility.

Above: The original patent drawings for the jet suit.

Left: A complete jet suit built from those early designs. This variant still had a pair of engines on each arm, but the leg engines had advanced up the legs to pause around the waist at the back. The electronics and batteries were slung around the front.

Above: Fuelling up with the wonderful open-minded folks at Harbour Air in Vancouver before TED 2017.

Below: Make or break: delivering the TED 2017 talk knowing that within twenty minutes of stepping off stage I'd be trying to fly live on the veranda.

Above: Behind the scenes in the setup room with my new best friend and impromptu ground support, Adam Savage.

Left: Stopping off at Boost VC in San Francisco, on the way to TED 2017, for the very first demo outside the Wiltshire farmyard — only to receive a $650,000 investment deal from Tim and Adam Draper, signed on this $100 bill (**below**).

Below: The later design of the jet suit with one large single rear engine, viewed from the back, with 3D printed aluminium arm engine assemblies and polymer printed backpack. This is one we sold.

Above left: Flying at the Farnborough International Airshow was a huge privilege and I felt an immense pressure to deliver at this world-renowned event, surrounded by the likes of BAE, Rolls-Royce and Lockheed Martin. It turned out to be a great event and it was a rush chasing around after our team Dodge Ram.

Above right: Flying the runway with the world-famous Red Arrows shimmering in my heat haze.

Below left: Me suited up, waiting for the green light from the tower to launch; a nerve-racking ordeal, trying not to think of the long list of technical issues that could ruin our day.

Below right: On day two the Spanish military pilots visited our stand and we made a deal to try and get a shot with one of their display Harriers hovering behind me. And that's what we managed to capture.

Above: To close out a highly successful three days at Farnborough in 2018, we decided to stage our first public display with two of us flying. With me on the left and Angelo on the right, we put on quite a spectacle.

Above left: Hammering along the waterfront at the Bournemouth Air Festival in 2018 with a lifeguard struggling to keep up.

Above right: Angelo and I pushed the limits of the engines at that event, knowing we had water and automatic lifejackets. It still made for some exhilarating plunges into the sea.

Left: Yet another honour: flying at the Royal Navy International Air Day in 2019, together with two of my other pilots, Sam Rogers and Dan Denham. It was a privilege for me to get the beret out. It was also quite an outing for Dan - a former RN Harrier and Sea King pilot, who had performed displays at this event for several years.

Left: An immense privilege to be invited back to a Royal Marines pass-out parade at Lympstone and flying the infamous Bottom Field Assault Course.

Above: Wing testing at speed off Hurst Castle on the south coast of the UK.

Below: Laying down the new Guinness World Record in 2019.

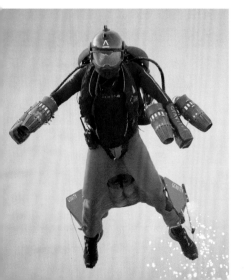

Above left: Special little boy Bailey. Having endured a lot of ongoing health challenges, he was guest of honour at the HMS *Sultan* STEM day.

Above right: One sure-fire way to get kids off their iPads is to capture their imaginations . . . by landing a 1,000 bhp jet suit at their school – here in Shanghai in 2019.

Below: Speaking in a stadium to 4,000 kids in Boston. The public response to Gravity has been phenomenal, and it's especially rewarding to see children and teenagers getting excited by what we are doing.

Left: The collaboration with Adam Savage which saw me fly a 'real' Iron Man suit printed in titanium.

Below: Early days of multiple pilot flights around water obstacles at Lagoona Park in Reading, paving the way towards the International Race Series. It's quite simply the most intensely exhilarating thing I or my pilots have ever done. It truly is like that dream of flying.

pilots, BMXers and edge-of-the-atmosphere freefalling skydivers, the company had created a distinct and powerful image for themselves, and somehow without the usual catalogue of deaths and PR disasters. Meanwhile, their videos carried an air of authenticity and daredevil expertise that other brands lacked. Everyone who watched a run-of-the-mill trials bike rider as he raced towards the edge of a cliff at full pelt usually experienced the same reaction: that a clumsy, possibly amateurish and gory ending was inevitable. Protect that same trials bike rider with a Red Bull crash helmet, however, and the perspective shifted dramatically: the video became a death-defying thrill ride pushing human capability to new limits. I definitely wanted to land in the latter category.

After several meetings with Red Bull's creative team I'd shown enough to prove the worth in Gravity Industries' debut product and they agreed to make a short on the jet suit. Their film crew later captured a series of clips that combined my unusual working practices: those middle-of-the-night 40km runs, a torch strapped to my head; interviews and snapshots of workshop activity and gym work; and eventually I was filmed flying across the farmyard workspace, my breath misting in the freezing cold.

By that stage I had tweaked the jet suit so that the leg engines had migrated to just above my arse rather than resting against my calves, which created a bigger, wider curtain of thrust. The new design also prevented the engines from shredding the concrete floor of my test space, which had happened on a number of occasions, my turbines sometimes rendered inoperable by small chunks of broken stone that had exploded up into their workings. The good news was that with various adjustments my suit was now more reliable and capable than ever before.

I was working in San Francisco with BP when the Red Bull film eventually landed in my inbox. My stomach lurched. This, I knew, was a defining moment for Gravity Industries and the suit. Had the film carried the wrong feel, or misrepresented the ethos of my work, there was no way I could ask them for a second attempt. Everything had been filmed and edited, so my hopes for an exciting launch would be shattered. With the right tone, however, I could expect to be ushered through the same hallowed portals as some of the most inventive sports stars on the planet.

In a hotel room, jetlagged, my colleagues waiting downstairs, most of them still unaware of my weekend activities, I pressed play and sat back, the video clip loading to reveal a series of grainy, stylized images of my powering up the suit in the farmyard. There was the crunch of trainers as the cameras focused on the silhouette of my running form moving across the nearby fields in Salisbury. The tone was moody, emotive, as my voiceover described the motivations behind Gravity Industries. 'I've got this belief that the human mind and body is a pretty amazing machine,' I said off camera. 'And rather than putting that [body] into a machine, what about augmenting that *with* a machine? Just how far could we go towards reimagining human flight?'

As I watched, emotions raced through me. I'd sat through what I believed to be my live-or-die moment, *and I loved it*. It was as if a massive weight had been lifted from my shoulders. But the sensation was short-lived. Within a few days I'd come to feel slightly anxious again. Red Bull had mentioned they were planning on releasing the film on 31 March 2017, which meant a large number of people were likely to catch it for the very first time on April Fool's Day. The risk of my work being dismissed as a joke seemed high. But as the footage rebounded around the internet, the short movie gathered momentum. Calls came in from around the world; there were requests for interviews. The Associated Press website went into meltdown and within a week the Red Bull page dedicated to my short film had apparently gathered 'a billion impressions'. Though I was somewhat sceptical of that metric.

I also noticed something else was happening. My insecurities regarding Dad's demise had become amplified. Despite my successful launch and the fact that I'd just about maintained job security and had the promise of the investment money from Anthony, I felt nervous. I'd embarked on the same journey as Dad had. But with every passing day I tried to convince myself that this would be different. My best option was to press ahead.

My creation had been launched. Now all I had to do was cling on for the ride.

Workshop Notes

ALWAYS CONSIDER YOUR BRAND

Too many people disregard the idea of brand identity, instead focusing solely on the development of a product or idea. But human beings gravitate towards other personalities, symbols and stories far more quickly than a product. A brilliant innovation can be promoted very badly, without explanation, and will fail to reach the market in a successful way. It dies on the vine as a result. Alternatively, a mediocre idea can be positioned very clearly in the public's mind, with a clear story of what the product is, sometimes becoming a roaring success.

On a practical level, a strong brand identity also inhibits other companies from copying the product. A company such as Burberry might have been overrun by competitors mass-producing cheaper imitations of their tartan bags and scarves. However, the style in which their brand was established meant they've been regarded more highly than their rivals. I know a firm in China could quite easily have copied what Gravity Industries have been doing with the jet suit. Without an authentic identity I might have been lost in the competition, but our brand personality has helped secure our position within the minds of the public.

Takeaways

- Take time to build the brand. Remember, having a great idea is only the start. So much more work goes into locating a route to market, establishing the right messaging, and putting in place commercial infrastructure. It's important we take the time to invest in these aspects.

- Always think about how a product is launched. Once an innovation has been unveiled it's impossible to put the genie back in the bottle. We must always consider brand identity, ensuring the product release chimes with our key values.

- Always fight to survive. In the darkest times an inner critic will emerge that urges us to listen to the doubters. Consider the Special Forces soldier. If we have belief in the fact that what we're doing is worthwhile, drown out pessimism with self-belief and press ahead.

12

BE YOUR OWN SUPERHERO

Or, What to Do When Financial Opportunity Comes Calling

There are times in innovation and business when we have to hold our nerve under pressure. Often that moment takes place as we're taking our first steps, when interest arrives from an outside source. This might present itself as a potential investor, or our first customer looking to make a long-term order. It's at these moments that our self-value is sometimes challenged: *is our idea, or product, as valuable as we believe it is?* Finding the balance between striking a successful deal and selling the product or concept short is often tricky, and it's important we think and act in a calm manner when making that decision. Rash judgements can lead to long periods of regret.

My dilemma arrived as word of the jet suit spread. Much of my newfound profile, and that of the suit, had everything to do with a TED Talk I delivered in April 2017. In that nervy period between filming with Red Bull and *Wired*, and their resulting footage placing Gravity ever-so-slightly on the map, I decided to get in touch with Chris Anderson, the owner of TED – Technology, Entertainment, Design, an online resource that posts brief but informative presentations by fascinating people, including military vets, world record holders, and innovators in science and business. Notable TED alumni include Bill Clinton, Al Gore, Professor Stephen Hawking, Elon Musk and Bill Gates. Meanwhile, TED Talks videos are often watched by millions of people online and tend to act as a launch pad for characters embarking upon very interesting journeys. This was a community I wanted to connect with.

I decided to take the plunge.

Having made a tenuous link with Chris via a mutual friend, and emboldened by the media interest in the jet suit, I reached out with the emailed equivalent of a cold call, though my note came across as quite vague. I was still holding my cards close to the chest when it came to the exact workings of the suit. At the time Red Bull were yet to release their online film, and I wanted to maintain an element of surprise.

> **Richard@Gravity:** Hi Chris! I have an idea TED might quite like to hear about. I can't really tell you that much about it just yet because it hasn't been fully launched, but it's this quite audacious story of trying to fly something unusual, while working on a human mind–body relationship. I wonder if it would be cool to do something with you guys? I love TED and I've been listening to your talks, often while I've been running . . .

Chris and his team must have received thousands of emails in that vein, general enquiries and requests that lacked any real focus. I was probably rambling and a little incoherent, but to his credit he responded fairly quickly.

> **Chris@TedTalks:** Thanks Richard. OK, great. Well, you'll have to tell me more otherwise I won't know what you're talking about.
>
> **Richard@Gravity:** So, I've been flying this thing that a lot of people think is like an Iron Man suit. There are a lot of ways I can spin the story if you were to give me the time on TED: there's the endeavour, the journey, the dream of flight, and a sense of overcoming adversity. All the things that usually go down so well on the videos . . .
>
> **Chris@TedTalks:** All too clichéd. That's been done before, countless times. We need something different . . .

191

I made one last attempt to explain, loosely, what I was trying to achieve. But Chris's response stopped me in my tracks: 'Not getting it.' I realized I'd approached a point where my emails might soon become annoying. I was also keen not to appear desperate in any way.

> **Richard@Gravity:** Chris, I'll stop wasting your time. Let me launch this thing and then if the world likes it I can come back to you and better describe what's been happening. Loved chatting to you. Richard.

Our conversation was done. But shortly after the release of the Red Bull video, I received another email from Chris. This time his tone was markedly different.

> **Chris@TedTalks:** Oh my God, Richard, I'm really sorry – I get it. Please accept my apologies on not recognizing you sooner. What you've done is absolutely awesome. And yes! Please, please come to TED 2017 in three weeks. It's in Vancouver and we'll pay for all your expenses . . . By the way, is there any chance you could fly the suit while you're over there? That would be incredible!

I scanned the email and dropped it into the folder marked 'Unread'. I closed my laptop, opened my wardrobe for a pair of trainers and went running, my brain attempting to process exactly what had happened. *I was only going to do a TED Talk!* Even better, I was a guest speaker at TED 2017, a five-day conference set to take place that April, comprising talks on technology, entertainment and design, as well as global issues, science and the arts. Seventy speakers had been scheduled to appear and among them were the likes of self-described 'Human Guinea Pig' Tim Ferris, His Holiness Pope Francis, maverick businessman Elon Musk and chess grandmaster Garry Kasparov. I was to share the stage with a pantheon of great minds. My head spun. *What the hell would I say?*

I needn't have worried about the structure of my talk too much. Prior to my arriving in Vancouver it was arranged that I should chat to Chris over Skype. He wanted to get a feel for how I'd arranged my presentation and, having watched a ton of TED Talks, I was fairly confident in my ability to deliver an entertaining narrative that retold the story of my journey. In my head I'd worked up a sound structure, and I'd drawn together plenty of amusing videos from my prototype phase. There were shots of me testing the first engine on a country lane, shots of me falling over in the farmyard, trying multiple proto-types, and so on. But when I dialled into TED, to my horror I was greeted with the sight of a room full of people looking back at me, all of them armed with clipboards and pens. In the middle of this intimi-dating collective was Chris.

'Hi Richard,' he said, smiling reassuringly. 'Let's go through your talk. We love what you've done with the jet suit. Now lead us through your backstory.'

I retold the tales of my many failures while building the suit. This led to a series of approving nods and a period of frantic note-taking. This, I hoped, represented a promising start.

Chris listened intently throughout. 'That's really cool, Richard, but there's something missing,' he said, having thought on it for a moment. 'We need a human story. Men of pretty much any age will love the horsepower and flight stories, but how does the "soccer mom" fall in love with this? Why would she give a crap about watching a video on someone making a jet suit?'

I had one more card up my sleeve, but I had felt very reluctant to play it.

Dad.

I understood there was a powerful connection between the values of innovation instilled into me and my father's love of flying and science. His subsequent demise certainly delivered an emotional backdrop to my work and provided a huge amount of motivation, but it was a highly sensitive issue and I wondered how my retelling of his troubles might affect me. I swallowed my concerns and went ahead, unravelling to the TED team the details of what had been a very emotional childhood experience, and explaining my route to creating what was now viewed as an innovative product and the process's traumatic hue, having previously lived through the consequences of Dad falling short.

Chris and his team of clipboards nodded sympathetically.

'That's it, Richard,' he said, once I was done. 'That's the human element that will resonate with people. Everyone has lost someone and people can connect with that.'

I was almost there.

They say you make your own luck, which is true, though I'm not so sure of the practical science behind that thought. What I do know is that a person has to strike when good fortune comes their way. The moment has to be seized. My understanding of this was crystallized by a smattering of experiences as I worked on the suit. One notable event took place once I'd booked my place on TED 2017 when I was contacted, out of the blue, by venture capital investor Adam Draper. The connection would soon turn out to be the first in a brilliant chain of events.

Adam's father, Tim, had previously launched the Draper University of Heroes, a facility based in San Mateo, California, that delivered a course in 'entrepreneurship'. Adam, meanwhile, was the co-founder and managing director of Boost VC, a company investing in unique start-ups and ideas looking 'to make sci-fi a reality'. His personal page on the Boost VC website imparted several fascinating snippets of intelligence, including the revelation that 'in a previous life, he wanted to be a professional tennis player and has an odd affinity for Australians. He once drank an entire bottle of Tabasco sauce (the big ones) in 43 seconds.' Most exciting for me, though, was the news that 'no idea is too crazy. He dreams of building an Iron Man suit and leads the deals in the wildest sci-fi tech investments – exoskeletons, jetpacks, rockets . . . Go big or go home.'

Strangely, I hadn't heard of Adam prior to his email inviting me to fly to California, where he wanted me to do a display for his team. At that time I hadn't flown anywhere other than the farm. I was still a fairly under-the-radar concern, and the idea of travelling around the world while making money from shows and private performances hadn't really occurred to me. But this was an opportunity too good to miss.

'This guy is either a lunatic or a genius,' I thought. '*I'm going . . .*'

Given my inexperience when it came to taking the suit on foreign adventures, I had very little in the way of infrastructure or equipment for transporting a collection of jet suit parts that, when laid out on the table of Homeland Security, looked not too dissimilar to a thermonuclear device as portrayed in a series of action films. The two enormous Pelican cases I eventually ordered to transport the first suit weren't unlike the sort one might expect a shipment of M-16 assault rifles to arrive in had they been smuggled over the border by a well-organized arms trader. Unsurprisingly, the lady at the check-in desk at Heathrow was not impressed.

'Hmmm, they're not going to fit on to the conveyor belt,' she said, eyeing my luggage suspiciously. 'You'll have to spread the load across more suitcases.'

Talk about a terrible start. There I was, preparing my first public flight before a team of Silicon Valley influencers, making a last-minute dash to The Suitcase Store, where I suffered the indignity of shoving various bits of my jet suit into a new bag, shaking my head over the fact that my fancy cases had weighed 10 kilos each even when empty. What's worse, there was a list of issues to deal with when I arrived in the US. Due to some technical difficulties I was without two of my micro turbine engines and had been forced to pre-order a set from an American supplier. I spent the entire flight praying that my instructions had been followed to the letter. I'd also been rushed into some sketchy last-minute repairs, having noticed a small hole in the suit's fuel tank: with the help of a clamp I'd pinched the wound shut. The most troubling glitch, however, was an electronics failure that I'd been unable to resolve prior to leaving the UK, which would have to be repaired once I landed.

Undeterred, I eventually made it to San Mateo the following day – my equipment made it through airport security somehow – where I was ushered into the Boost VC offices, a typically trendy set-up comprising plush sofas, virtual-reality test areas, and at the heart of it all a giant mural featuring fictional caped and un-caped crusaders, including Batman and Superman.

'Holy amazing opportunity, Batman!' proclaimed Robin, Bruce Wayne's junior sidekick, in one image.

Alongside him, a lasso-twirling Wonder Woman echoed Boost VC's inspiring mantra: 'Unleash the heroes!'

I stared at the colourful imagery, the company's adventurous spirit slowly sinking in. 'Oh, I get it now,' I thought. 'God, I hope I can pull this off.'

Walking towards me was Adam, an enthusiastic thirty-something multi-millionaire desperate to see the suit's inner workings. Not that there was too much to show at first. My engines had arrived, thank God, though given my surroundings I'd only get the chance to test them properly in front of a crowd of very influential and seriously rich people. I'd already worked through the night, correcting my electronics failure while coming to terms with what would later become a vital component of the suit – a new helmet gifted to me by Daqiri, the company responsible for manufacturing equipment featuring the innovative heads-up display system, the fancy piece of kit that allowed me to keep an eye on my speed, fuel consumption and altitude in-flight on a display positioned inside the visor. As a one-off item it typically cost around $15,000, but I was totally inexperienced when it came to using one. Just looking through the visor felt strange. A series of digits appeared before my eyes as I moved and it all seemed very sci-fi, like a POV scene from the Arnold Schwarzenegger movie *The Terminator*. More worryingly, the helmet, a version of which was usually worn by industrial machinery operators, weighed 1.5 kilos: should I fall or land badly, the whiplash as my head banged against the ground was likely to be considerable. I prayed for a secure launch.

As the sun rose, I started the day by warming a 20-litre bag filled with diesel, leaving it out in the sun – a process that gave me the maximum chance of starting up my as-yet-untested engines (starting the jet suit with cold fuel is like starting a car on a very chilly day). The moment of no return had arrived, and a small crowd, led by Adam, strode towards me in the car park of Boost VC as I powered up the turbines. *One, two, three, four, five.* The four arm turbines began to idle with a reassuring burst of noise. Then my heart sank. One of the untested rear engines, delivered not twelve hours previously, was lifeless. I sensed a mood of confusion among the audience as I paced around nervously, hoping, praying, my luck might change.

'I'm just warming up,' I shouted in a desperate attempt to style out what was a potentially humiliating situation.

I needn't have stressed. There was a cough, a splutter, then a reassuring rush of power as my new equipment trembled and ignited, the down force whipping up a typhoon of dust and grit as I slowly rose into the air. I must have lifted only 6 or 7 inches from the ground, but I zipped over the tarmac for 30 seconds or so, dirt particles blowing away in my slipstream, and it was enough to impress the various Silicon Valley execs gathered together to watch what had somehow, miraculously, been a successful demonstration. In the distance I even glimpsed a fire engine, its crew staring open-mouthed as they filmed my flight on their mobile phones. There was a roar of applause when I landed and stowed my engines. A crowd gathered excitedly around me, including a tall, elegant-looking gentleman who seemed to be high-fiving Adam enthusiastically. He approached me with a smile on his face, a one-hundred-dollar bill in his hand. And then I recognized him as Tim Draper, Adam's father, the billionaire head of one of the longest-standing dynasties in Silicon Valley.

'That was the most awesome thing I've seen,' he shouted over the hum of the engines' cooling cycle, diesel fumes choking the air. 'Here you go, here's your first revenue as a start-up because you've cleaned out all the dust and dirt from my parking lot.'

Laughing, I sensed a pivotal moment in Gravity's progression arriving. If I had been capable of impressing the impossible-to-impress, an investor who had presumably seen it all during his time in the Californian start-up race, then what did that mean for me and the jet suit? I tried my best to remain composed, even as I noticed that Tim and Adam had moved away from the crowd and were chatting excitedly. Was something interesting about to happen?

Adam stepped forward.

'Richard, our ethos as a family and as a firm has always been "To be your own superhero",' he said. 'That's what we believe it takes to succeed. We have to be part of this. How do you fancy half a million dollars for a ten per cent stake in your company?'

I tried not to flinch. The offer was undeniably a shock. The sum was mind-boggling. I paused and took stock. I had been so focused on the enormity of TED, the travel and the flight demo that I hadn't even considered investment. My sole intention when flying to San Mateo, ridiculous luggage and all, was to test the suit as a demonstration concept. I'd wanted to see how it might perform before a live audience, and I'd already achieved my goal. A large cash injection was an added bonus, so I had nothing to lose. But I wasn't looking to be greedy either. Then again, neither did I want to sell myself short: if people as influential as the Drapers were willing to hand over such a sum after what had been a fairly patchy demonstration, then how far would they be willing to go?

I drew in a settling breath.

'I wasn't really looking to raise money,' I said. 'But it would be fantastic to have you guys on board. How about half a million pounds, which is more like $650,000?'

Tim smiled. He was on a diesel-fumed high and had an admiring crowd sensing a legendary moment in the making. Pulling out a pen, he scribbled something on the hundred-dollar bill, passing back the note and shaking my hand enthusiastically.

'You have it, Richard,' he said.

When I looked down at the bill, I'd received an official offer, our 'contract' scribbled across the sour-looking face of Benjamin Franklin: '$650,000 for 10%'.

We were on. I later placed the note in a frame, which currently holds pride of place in the Gravity Lab – a reminder to myself that opportunity comes when you least expect it.

Workshop Notes

BE BOLD UNDER PRESSURE

Having to deal with the succession of challenges to execute that very first public flight was certainly daunting. I'd remained calm under pressure when it might have been very easy to crumble. Keeping focused on one problem at a time and methodically working through it had certainly helped. Much of that resolve had everything to do with my experiences in a pressured oil-trading environment, which also stood me in good stead when the unexpected Draper deal presented itself. By default I'd been a little sceptical within business settings, wary of saying yes to something I'd later regret. Prior to flying to San Mateo I hadn't considered the Drapers as an investment possibility. Their offer was a shock and easily could have caught me off guard.

My decision to accept only happened after performing a quick sense check. I asked myself if the Drapers seemed like reliable business partners – *they did*. I asked if they had a proven track record when working with innovative individuals – *that was very much the case*. And the money? Half a million dollars was a large sum, but I understood that the best offer rarely came in first. I pushed them a little bit, and it paid off.

Running a sense check can help all of us when operating in similar circumstances. Stop to think. Never say yes too quickly. Instead, take a little time to evaluate the situation and then act accordingly. Taking a little extra time and performing due diligence might be the difference between success and disappointment. I know it was for me.

Over the following week I built what I hoped was an entertaining and informative narrative for my TED Talk, detailing the suit's development while weaving in just enough of my tricky childhood to create a layer of context. I was careful not to pull too strongly on the heartstrings. The last thing I wanted was for people to feel sorry for me.

Once I'd landed in Vancouver, not long after meeting with the Drapers, TED assigned a 'mentor' to guide me around the facility and the infrastructure of the event. Otho was fantastic and eager to help me settle in.

'Do you want to chat to a friend of mine who gave a very well-received talk recently?' he asked. 'I mentored her last year. She went through a hell of a time learning how to connect with an audience. I think she was worried people might have had some pre-conceived opinions of her.'

Thinking it a very kind gesture, I asked who his friend was.

'Oh, her name's Monica . . . Monica Lewinsky.'

For those of you too young to know, or for readers unfamiliar with a scandal that dogged the Bill Clinton era of American politics, Monica Lewinsky is one of the most notorious figures in White House history. A former intern, Monica hit the headlines having been embroiled in an 'inappropriate relationship' with the leader of the Free World. Needless to say, it all ended very badly: Clinton was impeached and then acquitted of perjury and obstruction of justice; Monica became a pariah figure for a time.

Her TED Talk on 'The Price of Shame' had been a resounding success, however. And over dinner with Otho, Monica explained how her presentation had swayed public opinion; in a way it kick-started what would become a renaissance period in her life. She had been mocked by the American media for years. Somehow she'd survived, though apparently her talk proved she hadn't come away unscathed.

As I sat there, engrossed by an impressive story of recovery, my own surrealist adventure began to dawn on me. 'I'm about to do a TED Talk,' I thought. 'I've just raised half a million quid from one of the most influential VCs in Silicon Valley and now I'm having a beer with Monica Lewinsky.'

What the hell was happening to me?

Most of my pre-TED nerves hinged not on my talk but on yet another public display. In front of the likes of the Branson family, Al Gore and over twenty-one international media groups all intent on live-streaming, I was to run a live performance of the suit, which had proven a little unreliable in San

Mateo. No pressure. Thankfully, TED had given me every opportunity to ensure my display ran smoothly, and as I settled into the grand environment of a huge conference space a super-efficient stage assistant asked me for a list of working requests. I told her I'd need a set-up room and a table to prepare my equipment. She seemed to be communicating into some unseen radio. Every request was dispatched with an air of military precision and I was able to prepare, unencumbered by the risk of some person or backstage technical procedure messing with my best-laid plans.

There was a hitch, however.

I needed fuel, and had agreed to source my own once I arrived. In an event where immediacy was key, I didn't have the time to start and then restart the engines for hours on end, and I didn't want to risk someone else picking up the wrong fuel. My only problem was locating a stockist. Then it struck me: Vancouver harbour is a busy seaplane port and would surely have a supply of diesel – or better still, Jet A1 fuel. I was told that Harbour Air, a company famous for its seaplane tours in Canada, were the people to ask, so I picked up my fuel bag and set off. Having found my way to their building, which was situated past a line of iconic twin-engine Beaver seaplanes, I asked for whoever was in charge of the company's fuel supply.

'Sure, I'm the guy,' said one of the commercial managers. 'What can I do for you, buddy?'

I introduced myself as the inventor of a jet suit that he might have seen online, which thankfully he had. I then explained that I was about to present a live demonstration of my work to a conference audience with an online reach of several million people. The situation sounded so ludicrous when I said it out loud. There was some scratching of heads and then a flurry of activity. This was arguably the strangest request Harbour Air had received in quite some time. Minutes later I was back in the conference centre, my 20-litre bag of jet fuel under my arm.

With show time approaching, a nervous energy now crackled

about the place. I was sharing my set-up room with Cheetah, the famous robotic dog made by Boston Dynamics, but the team seemed a little edgy. Apparently, Cheetah had gone rogue at his last presentation, meandering offstage during a communication breakdown between man and mechanized beast, and the people from Boston Dynamics were understandably worried that a repeat performance might damage the company's reputation. With so much going on around me I tried very hard to play it cool, but the crazy vibe of what I was about to do seemed to increase by the hour. As I wandered the coffee area I came across none other than Adam Savage, the legendary costume engineer and presenter of TV show *Myth Busters*, who immediately proclaimed himself a fan of the jet suit. He was so enthused by it he offered to be my ground crew for the event.

And then it was go time.

My seven-minute talk kicked off in a blur, and with a fair amount of umming and ahhing as I explained the creative process behind my work.

'A small group of us got together to have a run at the whole challenge of flight that inspired people for years and do it in a very different way,' I said. 'And that's the journey I'd like to share with you now.

'The starting hypothesis was one of the human mind and body, which, as you've seen for the last few days here, is an amazing construct. What if you augmented that wonderful machine with just the right technology? If you approached flight in that kind of real way, where could you get to?

'I've got this vision. It sounds audacious, but let's just stick it out there, that one day maybe we can rise up above a beach, fly up and down the coastline of it, rise up a bit higher, with some of the safety kit we're working on to make this achievable. Then over the horizon comes a Hercules with the ramp down. As it comes past, you start picking up speed and see if we can intercept – from the rear, not the front, that would be a mistake – and then try and land in the back. And as I say, that's a little way off at the moment.

203

'This is also a very personal journey for me. Sadly, my father took his own life when I was fifteen, and left an awful lot of unfulfilled ambition. He was a wonderful inventor, a maverick creator. And I'd just like to think, if it was possible, if he was looking down, he'd certainly be smiling at some of the things we've done here. So, it's a tribute to him.'

I played some old test-flight footage. There was a raucous round of applause as I concluded my presentation and I should have been elated, but there was still nerve-racking work to do. Having left the stage, I was given a twenty-minute window in which to ready my kit, spool the engines and walk to a platform positioned outside, next to what was a famous statue of an orca whale built from black and white blocks. Named the Digital Orca, it had been designed by the famous Canadian artist and novelist Douglas Copeland and had looked rather cool as I'd wandered round the convention centre with my guide. Now my fancy launch pad resembled a hangman's gallows. The jet suit was a potential noose around my neck and my nerves were a little frazzled.

A well-meaning interviewer caught me as I left the conference stage to prepare my equipment, a camera trained on my face. For most people, completing a TED Talk was something of a career-defining moment; they often walked away carrying with them a sense of achievement and pride. But having been asked how mine had fared, I came across as somewhat tense. That was understandable: I was preoccupied, and the odds of me looking an idiot were uncomfortably short.

'That was the easy bit,' I said. 'I've got to fly a jet suit now.'

Vancouver can be terribly cold, even during springtime, and in the icy temperatures I had done my best to warm the fuel, praying that Harbour Air's Jet A1 would deliver first time. As I pulled on the throttle trigger, there was a high-pitched whine and then a slow burning roar as all my engines started at once. This should have been cause for cele-

bration, but I became instantly conscious of not wanting to make a misstep, or fall flat on my face in a humiliating display. As the engines reached idle and the launch lights turned green Adam gave me a smile. I squeezed the trigger and sensed a reassuring weightlessness, my feet drifting up from the ground. Knowing that an engine failure now would result in catastrophe for my career I made sure to avoid any painful tumbles as I left my launch pad by keeping to a relatively low altitude of several feet, cruising around my space in several turns. The raucous scream of my turbines ricocheted around the veranda, generating even more volume, which must have added to the dramatic scene. After a few more sharp turns I powered down, feeling the comforting solidity of concrete under my feet once more.

The sense of relief was overwhelming.

I had managed to secure a spot on the bill at TED 2017 and delivered a presentation of the suit's capabilities to more people than I could possibly imagine. I'd nailed a challenge that had been nothing more than a pipe dream a year earlier. In those days I'd known that what I was trying to do had the potential to be fairly special, but it was only the inkling of an idea and my ambitions had been fairly modest: I'd simply wondered, 'How cool would it be to lift off the ground, fly up over a farmyard wall, and come back and land in the same spot?'

Now everything had changed.

My world had changed.

And as I wandered, elated, through the TED Conference one last time to collect my stuff, stopping to say hi to Al Gore, the forty-fifth vice president of the United States, as he made coffee before chatting with the Apple creative responsible for inventing Siri, I had a sense that my parameters for success had shifted in a big way. TED, as it had been for so many other innovators in the past, had become my launch pad.

I could now aim higher – much higher.

Takeaways

○ Fortune favours the brave. I created a tenuous link to
Chris Anderson at TED Talks and ignored my insecurities
about whether he'd be interested in my work. Having
emailed him, I made sure not to be a pain in his backside
though. When it comes to contacting an influential person
cold, we have to ensure our actions don't become
unwelcome. Once we've annoyed someone it's so much
harder to engage about the future. Ask questions, but don't
be pushy.

○ Always seek support and advice from people who have
succeeded from a similar position to us. From my
perspective there was no better person to have as my
ground crew than Adam Savage, and it was hugely helpful
to discuss the execution of a TED Talk with Monica
Lewinsky. Her insights gave me confidence when it came
to connecting with an audience.

○ In moments when big decisions need to be made, always
run a sense check. Stop to think. Never say yes, or no, too
quickly. Evaluate the situation and then act on the results
of your analysis. At some point, though, you just have to
pull the trigger and take the plunge.

MISSION: POSSIBLE

Or, How I Continued to Learn
to Operate Under Pressure

When life throws us a curveball, such as a panicky flight in front of some of the most influential people in Silicon Valley, it's easy to flap. A sense of overwhelming panic can take hold and it becomes very easy for us to shut down and lose control when we need to be at the top of our game. This sensation is very common in sporting situations when moments of high stress push upon an athlete. It's the same in a dangerous job, such as the fire service, or police force. A paramedic might see somebody seriously injured in a horrific car crash and yet he or she will still have to work effectively.

To overcome any sense of panic, it's helpful to use a technique that calms the mind when people around you are losing theirs. Take in one or two deep settling breaths. This steadies the parasympathetic nervous system – our fight or flight response – allowing us to relax and seemingly get a handle on a situation that might be moving too fast. With that done, we can reconfigure, quickly settling on a new plan of action. Then we can press ahead with the next step, following through quickly and decisively.

The next time events seem to be spiralling out of control, use this technique. You'll be surprised at how much wriggle room it gives you during a situation that seems scary or volatile.

And following my appearance at TED 2017 I was being put under more pressure than most. Requests for flight demonstrations arrived thick and fast: Brazil, Canada, France, Germany, Italy, India, Spain, Singapore and the USA were checked off the list. The suit was in high demand. Closer to home I appeared at TEDx in Glasgow and at the launch of the STEM initiative in Manchester, a programme that promotes the learning of science, technology, engineering and mathematics in British schools – a campaign understandably close to my heart, given that it fosters the next generation of big thinkers.

But with all my travelling and air miles I soon learned about the trials and tribulations that a jet suit attracts as it traverses the world, even in a collection of suitcases. Usually issues emerged when boarding passenger aircraft – an act that I'm more than aware comes with a certain level of irony. After all, the writers at Marvel Comics only needed Tony Stark to pull on his Iron Man suit for him to travel to the other side of the planet. I can't recall him ever having to negotiate with airport security staff, the line of holiday makers behind him becoming increasingly disgruntled. If only he knew of the inconvenience.

At the time of writing we have clocked up events in over thirty countries. There have been times when I've had to transport my $440,000 suit via a courier because a member of airport security has freaked out about the smell of my equipment. On one such occasion I was travelling home from Germany, via Basel in Switzerland, where I had been performing a display at the annual show of an engine manufacturer I'd been working with. After some confusion about what I was trying to stow on the plane I was sent to a corner of the airport reserved for high-risk luggage carriers, where I stood like a naughty school boy as my bags were placed on to a high-tech scanner. In a twist of bad luck, the computer system then crashed. I was requested to open up my cases for a manual inspection, even though I'd attempted to speed up the process by showing officials a video of my suit in action. It had been a futile explanation of what was inside. Basel's security personnel seemed less than impressed and were low on humour.

'Open the suitcase,' said one guard sternly.

I flipped the catches on my case and stood back, watching as several slightly grumpy men viewed the various devices that, to their mind, probably resembled a fairly sophisticated IED. My heart sank. A whiff of petrochemicals tingled my nose. I had been running jet fuel through the suit during my demonstrations across the day in

Germany and hadn't found the time to flush it through properly. My bags now reeked like a Molotov cocktail.

'Well, that's not going anywhere,' snapped the fellow who seemed to be in charge of my inspection. 'It smells like gasoline.'

I tried to calm any fears by explaining that I'd been travelling with the suit for months, the fuel had been removed and it posed no risk in the hold. That only seemed to irritate the inspection team further. There was a period of tutting and head shaking. I was instructed to find another way of transporting the suit home.

One of the advantages of being something of a novelty in aeronautical terms was that several magazines had taken an interest in me, among them the in-flight publication of the very airline I typically travel with. Apparently, a number of pilots within the company had fallen in love with the jet suit idea. I'd even previously been able to call upon a captain to jump onside when I experienced some trouble at the check-in gates. He kindly explained to security personnel that he knew of me and the suit was perfectly safe to travel. My luggage was investigated so often that I stuck a laminated letter to the inside of each suitcase that said, 'Hi, me again!' The note then detailed the technology inside, along with a reassuring letter from airline officials outlining the perfectly harmless workings within. A lot of the time this has been enough to ensure a safe and comfortable passage through security. In Basel, however, the team on duty were clearly sticking to their guns. I was told to forget it. The suit was grounded and we were forced to secure its passage home via other means.

There are certain stresses that arrive with learning that a valuable possession might have to be left behind in an airport. The fear is that the people caring for it may not be 100 per cent diligent in its handling. I'm sure that anyone who's been parted from camera equipment or a bottle of pricey whisky for any given period could attest to the worry on the subsequent flight home. *Are my photographs going to be OK? Will my booze get swapped out for a cheaper brand?* So imagine leaving an item as unique as a jet suit – one that takes a lot of time and labour to construct, and costs more than a four-bedroom house in some British towns – in the hands of security staff at a Swiss airport. My stomach was in knots. But I shouldn't have been too concerned, as my super PA and wizard events-logistics organizer Katy swung into action behind the scenes. With about an hour to spare, I hailed a cab into the city to the nearest UPS depot and couriered my entire business back to the UK, making it back to the airport gate with a minute or so until the plane doors were due to close.

My heart rate was off the charts, but my suit was safe, travelling home on a separate flight. It was delivered to my workshop by a man-with-a-van within days.

The flipside of all these logistical challenges has been that my travels have brought me into contact with a huge range of amazing individuals. For example, during a recent visit to the States I was accosted by an intrigued fan of the suit who just so happened to be Pharrell Williams, the renowned rapper, music producer, fashion designer and business entrepreneur. I didn't recognize him at first. As I mentioned earlier, my interest in the world of popular music had started and finished with Michael Jackson's *Bad* in 1987. However, he seemed like a nice bloke and was very complimentary about my work, which was nice to hear.

One man who needed no introduction was Tom Cruise, the star of *Mission: Impossible*, *Top Gun* and *Cocktail*, and arguably one of the most famous movie stars on the planet. The circumstances behind my introduction to him were somewhat surreal. In 2017, with Tom promoting his latest film *The Mummy*, we were both invited to the studios of a Spanish TV show, the name of which translates roughly to 'The Anthill', where the production seemed to be a curious mix of *Tomorrow's World* and *The Graham Norton Show*, with celebrities and incredible gadgets brought together under one roof. For this

211

particular episode I was the technological element, which led to a surreal moment in the show's green room where I waited, kitted out from head to toe in Gravity technology, knowing that I was about to perform for Tom Cruise himself and his two glamorous co-stars from *The Mummy*, Annabelle Wallis and Sofia Boutella. The idea was for me to demonstrate the capabilities of the jet suit to the viewers and one of the most influential actors in cinematic history. To say I was nervous would be something of an understatement.

When the offer of appearing on 'The Anthill' had first come through, I wasn't entirely convinced I should go. The jet suit, while advancing in reliability, was still an early version, and I hadn't been 100 per cent sure of pulling off a TV performance at that time. I didn't want to appear on a slew of TV cock-up compilations with a comedian making wisecracks over the top, my fledgling career as an innovator confined to the scrapheap of YouTube funnies. The production team also told me they wouldn't be able to pay for my appearance, and the trip would take up valuable time we didn't have. But then I was presented with an intoxicating kicker.

'Richard, Tom Cruise is going to be the other guest,' revealed a producer.

Though I am generally unfazed by celebrity, the thought of being introduced to Tom seemed hugely appealing, especially given his well-known love of speed, power and flight. Among Tom Cruise's fleet of vehicles were a Bugatti Veyron, which was able to accelerate from 0 to 60 in 2.4 seconds, a Vyrus 987 C3 4V bike, a WW2 Mustang fighter plane and a Gulfstream Jet that his ex-wife Katie Holmes described as being like 'a bus, only quicker' (a bus worth $20 million, which was a present for Holmes). If all else failed, I would at least have planes, trains and automobiles to fall back on as a conversational icebreaker.

The show, when I arrived there, was every bit as chaotic and crazy as I had anticipated. The studio was decorated with all sorts of memorabilia from *The Mummy*. There were mocked-up pyramids and palm trees, all of which looked very fragile. At one end was a raised platform and it was hoped that I could lift off from there as the show's presenter and his prestigious guests watched from a Perspex box positioned at the opposite end of the room. The interviews seemed to go on for ever, and though I'd brought my father-in-law, a retired engineer, along for moral and technical support, I was feeling distinctly nervous. He had watched in the past with awe and amusement as I'd blown around the farmyard with various prototype engines strapped to my body; there were many times when he'd been called upon to help gather together the remnants of my suit following a failed flight, or to hold up a fuel tank as I tried to power the turbines. I'd thought it might be rather fun for him to come along on what was a prestigious trip. But neither of us had experience of operating under such pressures.

Thank God the show wasn't live.

Tom, Annabelle and Sofia were ushered into their protective see-through box – a legal precaution, I suspect – and a member of the production crew gestured for me to start with a thumbs-up.

'Oh my goodness!' shouted Annabelle, peering into the gloom at the noisy non-event taking place at the other end of the studio. 'How fabulous! Of course it would be a British person . . .'

I was running the original six-engine suit (I had yet to progress to the five-engine suit that would arrive with later designs) and I was fuelled by some locally sourced diesel that I could only hope was up to standard. I powered up the engines, the sound ricocheting around the studio like a fleet of fighter jets taking off at once. But then to my horror nothing happened. The lights on my control system informed me that one of my engines was failing during start-up. My heart sank. There was nothing for it but to shut down the rest. I wanted to dig a hole and jump into it.

With the engines powering down, Tom tried to approach me. 'Oh, I've seen this suit!' he shouted, before being guided back into his protective box, ear defenders placed around his head.

I soon realized that the studio's rather warm ambient

temperature – it was thirty degrees – was likely to be killing my thrust. I'd also made the mistake of leaning forward to check the information lights on the electronic control panel on my chest. That meant the fuel inlet manifold, which takes the liquid to the engines, possibly wasn't drawing on the fuel needed to power my turbines. The problem was fixable, but I needed a little more time.

I turned to the producers, nervously. 'Give me five minutes to get this going,' I said, not really knowing how long I needed. 'I *will* get this going.'

I continued to fret. I'd heard that Tom Cruise was notoriously impatient, that he rarely suffered fools gladly and, given his tightly packed schedule, often had a cavalcade of blacked-out cars and a private jet on standby that could whisk him from meeting to meeting in double-quick time. I was now in danger of impinging on his plans and the 'TC' support team were becoming visibly anxious. But to my surprise he seemed very relaxed about the delay.

'There is no problem at all,' he shouted. 'We've got as long as you need. *I want to see this!*'

And he disappeared back to the green room for a coffee.

Now I was really staring down the barrel of a gun – it was do or die time. I swapped out my batteries and fixed the fuel issue, but my main problem was the temperature: I'd been running the engines for so long that the turbines had produced an insane amount of hot air in a room that was already very warm. Luckily, a restart period was enough to resolve my issues. The equipment roared back to life, the cameras rolled again, Hollywood's A-list returned to their viewing box, and I managed to complete two flights across the studio floor, the room filling with diesel fumes as I moved.

When I touched down the second and final time, Tom burst from the Perspex box, holding out his hand. 'That was amazing!' he yelled over the idling engines. I was so taken by the gesture that I completely forgot to acknowledge the show's presenter standing alongside him, who was apparently quite a big deal in European TV circles. I found myself performing a somewhat awkward double handshake with the two of them. Tom had gripped my hand so tightly that I was a little taken aback. Our faces told two very different stories. My eyes brimmed with relief. *Holy crap, I can't believe I've pulled this off!* Tom's face was lit up with a childlike exhilaration. *Oh my God*, his expression seemed to say, *this is jet engines and horsepower and flying. This is so awesome!*

We must have talked for around ten minutes, Tom hitting me with queries about recirculation, thrust generation, power-to-weight ratios and compressor designs. His enthusiasm was fiery and contagious.

'I'd love to try this,' he said eventually. 'My people will contact you – I *will* follow up on this.'

'The Anthill', despite my reservations, had been a success. Tom was true to his word, too. *Mission: Impossible*'s stunt coordinators got in touch regarding the jet suit and its use in a future movie, as did James Bond's production team, though both crews had worked on their upcoming films a little ahead of my schedule. I wasn't quite ready, but given those conversations in 2017, Gravity is now immersed in the Hollywood community. Watch this space.

Although not from Tom Cruise, we have had endless requests to sell suits to people since we launched the company. But I'm aware that we need to exercise a huge amount of caution when selling the equipment to wealthy people who may or may not fly with the right level of care and caution. We simply won't sell a person a suit until we've seen they are capable of flying it responsibly. For now, the price tag has acted as a pretty good filter: it's unlikely a random troublemaker will purchase the suit on a whim, given that it costs the same amount of money as two-and-a-bit Aston Martin DB11s. Instead we currently run training sessions from our flight laboratory to check a person's capability; certain skills and flight procedures have to be taught. So far, two private owners of the suit have asked to store their equipment with us, dropping in to use it whenever they're near by. This has worked pretty well – the last thing we'd want is for a wealthy or

high-profile figure to buy a suit and hurt themselves or others by flying in an inappropriate location.

I n November 2017, Guinness wanted me to appear and set a record
as the main event of their World Records Day, an annual event
displaying all sorts of wonderful feats of ground-breaking dex-
terity, velocity and exertion. Their plan was to have me set a
world record for the 'fastest speed in a body-controlled jet engine
suit'. But Guinness also give a spotlight to some of the more eccentric elements of world record-breaking. In 2015, a skateboarding
dog had taken centre stage. A year later the headlines had been
dominated by a biscuit-dunking bungee jumper who hurled himself from a great height and dipped a cookie into a mug of tea as his
cord flexed. Given my concern at being portrayed as a Doc Emmett
Brown type (the hyperactive inventor from *Back to the Future*), I
wasn't too keen at first. After the Red Bull and *Wired* publicity I had
pedalled hard in order to avoid an association with terms such as
'wacky' and 'eccentric'.

'This isn't us,' I explained to the Guinness representative. 'Think
Tony Stark, Elon Musk and the US Navy SEALs. We're not the next
skateboarding dog. I love the *Guinness Book of World Records*, but this
has to be sincere and audacious.'

I was assured that Guinness intended to present the attempt with
an air of seriousness, and that their desire to have the jet suit at the
event *was* extremely sincere. Apparently they had previously featured
high-end performances with brands such as Mercedes. In the end, I
caved. 'Oh sod it,' I said. 'Let's do this. Find a stretch of water so I can
fly safely and I'll attempt to set a time.'

My world record attempt was seat-of-the-pants stuff; it became a
live research and development exercise. I had no real idea of the
speeds attainable by the suit and I hadn't put any thought into how

best to push the suit's limits because doing so over land would have been rather dangerous. When the day eventually arrived, it suddenly felt like quite a big deal. Given my busy schedule in the build-up I had barely done any preparation and wasn't sure of being able to execute a suitable flight time. When I got to the designated lake in Reading called Lagoona Park I was suddenly under the watchful gaze of dozens of cameras, drones and smartphones owned by various members of the Guinness team.

No pressure, then.

A chap from the *Guinness Book of World Records* pointed out the course over which I was to travel. The plan was to fly from shore out over the lake and around a large buoy at the other end, banking as I approached the turn, returning to my original position in the quickest possible speed over a set distance of 300 metres. Given that nobody had attempted this stunt before, I was set to have my name in the hallowed tome alongside the world's tallest man even if I didn't fly particularly quickly. That didn't stop me taking a keen interest in the details, however.

I strapped on the suit and stepped towards the water's edge for a couple of practice flights. The weather was less than ideal. Cold and drizzly, it was a typically British November day. And as I rose from the ground, another elemental factor came into play. A hefty crosswind buffeted my arms as soon as I'd gathered speed, causing me to experience a significant and disconcerting lateral yaw. Drifting over the water, I reached the turn with a fair degree of speed but managed it all the same, the odds of a disastrous failure now shortened considerably. Luckily, my suit was equipped with a life jacket designed to inflate upon first contact with water. Not so luckily, I hadn't found the time to test its reliability. Were I to make a splashy mess of this world record attempt, I'd have to hope the safety equipment operated under pressure.

There had been yet another, more terrifying problem to deal with. During that first test flight I had taken off with way too much fuel for a run based on speed rather than distance. I'd been deliberately

217

conservative to avoid the possibility that the engines might run out halfway round, dropping me into the water like a stone. But with so much weight strapped to my body I was never going to set a quick time. With the fuel load reduced on the second run, maintaining a steady altitude had become a real issue. As I turned around the buoy, burning fuel and shedding weight by the second, I found myself climbing higher, much higher, and I drifted skywards to well over 60 feet, my speed increasing too.

My brain worked through some rapid calculations. 'Right, I've got two problems here,' I thought. 'I'm too high and I need to lose velocity to land safely, but I can only fix one issue at a time.'

In a split second, and with landfall looming, I reduced my speed, holding position over the beach at one end of the lake as my head whirled. *I've never climbed to this altitude in the suit before!* Falling now would result in a serious injury. Cautiously I released the trigger slightly and edged towards land. My adrenalin spiked; I vectored up and down in a jerky fashion, a life of unbridled curiosity flashing in front of my eyes as I thankfully began to descend and nervously reached the floor. The stressful landing had probably lasted only a few seconds, but felt like hours.

One of the Guinness team came rushing over and enthusiastically told me I'd recorded a speed of 32 mph. I was pleased but it felt faster, and I knew that I could have a crack at bettering it on the next run – but maybe after a cup of tea.

Some twenty minutes later I was spooling up again, this time with the suit power adjusted to reduce any unwanted lift. I launched aggressively and shot off at what felt like a real rate of knots, skimming low over the water. The marker buoy loomed and I vectored hard to the side to execute a rapid turn, barely noticing that I'd dropped perilously close to the lake's surface. I was now only a couple of metres from the water and my height was decreasing. Then I felt the uncomfortable sensation of wet feet.

'I'm going in,' I thought. 'Oh bloody hell . . . *I'm going in.*'

My body and suit submerged. The engines choked and instantly stalled as they went under. I hung in the water for a second or so.

'Well, this is new,' I thought. 'How do I get out of this?'

With a bang, the life jacket deployed, pulling me upright until, somewhat embarrassingly, I realized I'd landed in only 4 feet of water and was perfectly capable of standing up without the assistance of a self-inflating buoyancy vest, or the jet ski that was speeding towards me. I stood at the water's edge, dripping wet, posing with my thumbs up for the book's official photographer, delighted to have set a world record and simultaneously pondering.

Workshop Notes

ENJOY THE VICTORIES

Passing over successes too quickly, focusing only on what needs to be done or improved, is a trait of most innovators, or creative minds. For example, successful movie directors rarely recall the numerous and glowing reviews for their work; instead they focus on the lone bad one. Likewise, when we're working on an ambitious project, sometimes we're so keen to move forward we forget to enjoy the latest achievement.

I had just set a Guinness World Record, a success that would have seemed impossible to me as a child. The event had been filmed for a worldwide audience, and though I'd crashed, my minor failure had been offset by the fact that my safety equipment had worked well under stress. Within hours I was appearing on ITV, ITN, BBC, breakfast TV and Sky. Suddenly Gravity was all over the media again.

And yet all I felt was relief at having not made a fool of myself. I'd got so caught up with how I would be perceived that I'd lost sight of the fact that a credible story for myself had already been written through my earlier launch. I needn't have worried what the rest of the world thought at the *Guinness Book of World Records* event because my emergence had already been successful, thanks to coverage from Red Bull, *Wired* and TED.

Instead I should have enjoyed the victory more – if only for a moment. Doing so gives us the motivation and confidence to glide into the next challenge more easily.

n all the events I've completed so far, I've never had a serious problem. *Touch wood.* I'd like to think this is down to the near obsessive level of preparations I go through before every event. I pore relentlessly over the performance of the suit. I triple-check everything. I'm naturally obsessive anyway, so when something doesn't look or sound right I examine it to an excruciating level of detail because it's my backside hanging out if things go wrong.

I check the intricacies of the flight path that I'm intending to take, because in the early days this was something that could create problems. I'd arrive at an event, a series of people running around anxiously as I prepared my equipment, and in all the chaos it often became easy to accept a flight route that was unsuitable. I'd stand on my launch platform looking out at the runway of an airfield or a racetrack wondering, 'Why do they want me to go there?' Now I make sure I have my route worked out well in advance. When I was preparing to fly at the Farnborough Airshow, I even got together with my two sons the night before and we built a Lego model of the runway and filmed a stop-motion animation of the flight plan.

Once I'm walking from my holding area to the start point of a demonstration it's easy to become intimidated by the experience, a bit like a musician walking out on stage or a scuba diver as they're about to drop into the water. There's a lot of highly technical equipment in place and there's a myriad of things that might fail. There have been times when my equipment has gone wrong in the seconds leading up to take-off, which often elicits a flurry of panic from the organizers. On those occasions I remain really quite calm as I focus on solving the problem, swapping out the electronics control system or batteries. That often takes no longer than ten minutes.

At Gravity we endeavour to be prepared for every possibility – good and bad. On one occasion, in 2018, I was invited to travel to South Africa after meeting Dr Peter Diamandis, the founder of Singularity University and one of *Fortune* magazine's '50 Greatest Leaders' – a man who counts space industry, entrepreneurship and 'abundance' among his specialist subjects. Having been introduced to Peter in San Francisco, where I'd proudly showed off the jet suit, I was asked to repeat the display in Johannesburg shortly afterwards, though this left me with a problem of the aeronautical variety. As any airline pilot will know, the South African city is particularly tricky to take off from because of its altitude: Johannesburg is situated 1,700 metres above sea level. The summer months are also very hot. This combination means that the air density there is very low, making it difficult for planes to leave as their engine performance is degraded in those conditions, which is why the airport has one of the longest runways in the world: planes need more distance to gather the additional speed required to lift away into the sky.

As air becomes heated it reduces in density, which is why hot-air balloons rise. Meanwhile, at altitude air gets thinner, which is why mountain climbers struggle to breathe. These two factors combine to affect jet engines. In a place like Johannesburg they don't have as much air mass to work with and for every revolution of the compressor there is a reduced mass of air, which is sucked in by the engines. Newtonian rules of physics are in play here: I blow air out of my engines at a very high speed, which is what thrusts me skywards. If the air is 20 per cent less dense, I lose 20 per cent of my thrust. As a side note, you might ask, 'Well, why do aeroplanes fly at high altitudes?' And while they do lose thrust at a great height, the reduction in aerodynamic drag from passing through thinner air more than compensates.

The realization of these potential altitude issues only struck me a week before I was due to fly. Apparently the very same altitude problem was set to strike my suit, but I was excited to fly in South Africa regardless of the technical headaches it might present me. I like showing up in new countries with different cultures; I can connect with new audiences, hear new ideas and share the Gravity story and our future plans.

As I prepared my equipment for the trip I decided to check in with my good friend Markus, who runs our engine-supplying partner, Jet Cat. 'Oh absolutely, you'll definitely lose power,' he said, with a worrying level of confidence. 'And it won't be just three or four per cent. There's twenty per cent less air density, so you'll lose twenty per cent power.'

I felt an unsettling sense of unease. The percentages were unnerving. If the suit produced a maximum 144 kilos of thrust, I would need to find another 30 kilos to compensate for the 20 per cent power loss in these conditions. The suit is often powered at 10 per cent less than its maximum power when I do display shows; if I'm doing a shorter flight I carry less fuel, which makes the suit lighter and therefore less demanding in thrust. But in Johannesburg, my maths wouldn't stack up. I didn't have an extra 20 per cent of power to play with. Then, when I realized the air temperature was set to be around 27°C upon my arrival, it dawned on me that I was potentially looking at a power loss of around 25 per cent. That sort of discrepancy might see me grounded in somewhat embarrassing circumstances, as 2,000 onlookers tutted and sighed at my spluttering engines.

As Dad had taught me during those endless hours in his workshop, part of the fun in science is making the seemingly impossible *possible*, and here I was presented with what appeared to be an insurmountable challenge. To my mind the odds were stacked against me, but rather perversely I began to relish the task – in a somewhat masochistic way – of tackling a monumental headache in calculation terms. There was an excitement to be found in surviving a precarious situation by the skin of my teeth. I quite enjoyed the idea of jamming my way through the problem, aided by a little bit of left-field thinking. However, my pragmatic, risk-averse planning style set me on edge. Failure was not an option, and the only way to ensure that my trip ended up a success was to lighten the suit's load. It was time to strip away some fat – on both man and machine.

I first removed the mesh covers that protected the arm engines, figuring I could get away without their assistance for a one-off display. I decided to run on only 7 litres of fuel for the flight, compared to the usual 12 litres, which should be enough whilst leaving some margin for error. I ditched my leather flight jacket, leaving me a little more exposed in the event of a fall, but it also meant there was one less kilo to fret about. But now I was maxed out on modification options. So I put on my trainers and ran.

On the day of my trip to South Africa, I prepped for the eleven-and-a-half-hour flight by skipping lunch and taking a 20-kilometre jog with the family dog. Jumping on the scales immediately afterwards, I learned that I'd shaved my bodyweight to 71 kilos – a statistic I maintained by eating very little on the flight, and for the next twenty-four hours I restricted my intake of food and drink, eventually seeking out a biltong shop in a nearby casino complex which made for a rather dissatisfying dinner. The following morning I ran the streets outside the hotel again. Then I ran some more. By losing several kilos in weight I estimated I had offset the 20 per cent loss in air density, and therefore thrust, meaning I was hopefully able to fly at the increased altitude without issue.

My physical and mental fortitude had taken a hammering. After just a few days of exercise and dedicated fasting I was in danger of going way below 70 kilos and the risk of passing out was suddenly real. There were one or two moments when standing up too quickly proved problematic. A strange blackness sometimes gathered in my peripheral vision and a dark circular tunnel appeared in my eyesight, the scene ahead of me closing in a rapidly decreasing circle before opening up again seconds later. It reminded me of those brief seconds before succumbing to a general anaesthetic. My problem was that I was experiencing the same unpleasant physical reaction simply by getting up from a chair. But the fear of failure was more worrying, and come flight time I had done enough to ensure my weight was on point.

My moment of truth had arrived. I stood on the launch platform in Johannesburg and felt a surge of relief as I squeezed the trigger to full power and slowly, but steadily, lifted away. And then a new challenge arose. Only a few feet into the air I experienced an awful flash of frustration: my heads-up unit and its electronic display had frozen. I was flying blind. This stress was amplified by the event organizers' plan for me to race down a Formula One track, pursued by a Porsche Cayenne. I was hardly taking on a basic flight. Once in the air I'd have to calculate the approximate time I had before my limited fuel reserves ran out and I dropped embarrassingly to the deck. Luckily my calculations were on point, and I soared over the tarmac, hovering above what was probably a pit-lane wall on race day, pausing for dramatic effect and landing ahead of the crowd.

Thank God I'd discovered the worrying details regarding Johannesburg and flight in the run-up to the event. Had I left everything to the last minute I would have found myself in trouble. Taking ownership of the most valuable parts of our work when preparing to perform under pressure is key. That doesn't guarantee that everything will work, but it certainly increases the chances. These days, the night before I fly at an event I usually get the equipment set up, running through everything apart from actually flying the jet suit. I believe that if I don't, and I leave it to only a few hours before flight time, something is bound to go wrong, in which case there wouldn't be the time to fix it.

I imagine a Formula One driver goes through a similar process: anyone who works with a system that's fast and dangerous has to be equally prepared. I'm sure they have a similar checklist before a race. They focus, they take responsibility; they get in the zone, ensuring everything has the best chance of running safely and successfully.

Of course, in my case a certain level of relief arrives immediately after a successful flight. That's usually when a spectator says to me, 'You've got the best job in the world, you must spend all day having a wonderful time.' The answer is: *Not really, most of the time there's just too much to think about; it's intense.* But for those few brief minutes in the air, once my preparations are done and I'm flying smoothly, the sense of complete freedom and exhilaration does make all the hard work more than worthwhile.

Takeaways

○ Remember the victories, they can give us the motivation we need to overcome the next challenge.

○ When under stress, take cues from an elite soldier: two deep inhalations, outline a plan, and then deliver on it.

14

RACE FOR THE PRIZE

Or, How Innovation Can Keep Me
Ahead of the Curve

W*hat's the point?*

For the first six months of my work on the jet suit, this was the question that plagued me the most. I'd meet someone interesting at a convention, our conversation would focus on horsepower and micro turbines; we'd discuss Heads Up technology and the future of flying. Then, mid-flow, I'd find myself reeling from what was a polite and genuine enquiry: 'It's great, but actually, where's this heading? *What's the point?*'

It was a question I'd ask myself too. What *was* the point? In the early phases of my work I didn't really have an answer other than the fact that I'd wanted to see a hunch through to the end, that the body was such an amazing instrument it might be possible to enhance a person with technology, thus reimagining the concept of personal flight. I had proved that theory pretty well. I hadn't set out on my journey with a clear idea of what I was going to do beyond that. I just did it, for the sheer joy of the challenge. *Because it was ludicrous and fun.*

Success had reframed my thinking, however. Having set world records and secured serious investment around the world, having showcased the suit at sixty-five events in twenty-one countries throughout 2017 and 2018, and projected Gravity Industries as a credible innovator, and having made it into *Time* magazine's list of 2018's best inventions, the time had arrived to consider what the next move should be, and how best to get there. I knew there were ways I might upgrade the current version of the jet suit. I also knew there were other versions of the suit the Gravity Team and I could explore as part of our research and development programme. Building on open-minded suggestions by Oliver and Thomas, one of these was the electric suit that could move underwater. There were even thoughts about developing various deployable wing systems, so that the wearer could glide at certain points in flight, saving on fuel expenditure, or maybe even use them as air brakes. All those ideas were too exciting to ignore. The trouble was, all of them required a steady stream of funding, especially if I was to take them beyond the early, magpie-like phases of R&D, which I knew would only get us so far as Gravity grew.

I knew one way of expanding our research and development budget was to continue delivering talks and flight events. These had been nice earners for the best part of eighteen months and had expanded people's awareness of Gravity to such an extent that I'd essentially been paid to do a global marketing campaign for the company. The downside of that particular tactic was that it consumed a lot of time and energy, which was a distraction from time spent in the lab with the team.

And then the solution dawned on me.

I pondered two distinct but potentially relevant innovations in recent history. I asked, *What's the point of a jet ski?* And, *What's the point of the Formula One racing car?* They were both entirely different creations, but both delivered thoroughly interesting lessons. In the case of the jet ski, it has a limited practical purpose other than to entertain the rider. The technology had hardly revolutionized the travel or maritime industries. Instead it presented tourists with yet another activity on their beach holiday, and speed enthusiasts with an aquatic variant of a motorbike.

Likewise the Formula One car: undoubtedly it is a feat of engineering genius, leading to spin-off technologies like ABS braking, but other than racing around a track at 200 mph for the entertainment of a global audience, what practical purpose does it fulfil? I began to realize that it was entirely acceptable for a company and an innovation to have the primary purpose of entertaining and inspiring audiences. Creating a spectacle that captures people's attention can be incredibly powerful, and can drive a significant revenue stream. Add in a healthy dose of human competition, exhilarating speed and high drama, and you have yourself an entertainment business, much like F1.

On Grand Prix weekends, fans flock to racetracks in their thousands; they gather around their TVs and in sports bars. People connect to different drivers and race teams. Other people gravitate towards the petrolhead aspect of the event or nerd out on the technology and performance stats. And there is a daredevil spirit in play. People really love the drama, the noise, the fear, the danger. Entertainment is all about visceral sensation. Two thousand years ago Roman gladiatorial combat was the en vogue entertainment. Muscle-bound men routinely did appallingly violent things to one another, and spectators couldn't draw their eyes away from the gory spectacle. Today, golfers, footballers, darts players and athletes all fight it out in a gentler way, but the psychology is the same.

Formula One has lost a little of its edge in recent years because the event has become too predictable and as a result has lost much of its drama. The same individuals win the Drivers' Championships; the same race teams lead the Constructors' Championships. And if we are to think honestly about our psychological motives for tuning in, the sport has also become a little too safe. The chances of seeing a driver leap from a flaming car or a wheel flying into the audience have rapidly diminished over the years – thankfully, of course; twenty-car pile-ups don't tend to happen and huge credit is due to the engineers for pretty much entirely eradicating the death toll that used to be associated with early motorsport. But as the dangerous aspect of the sport has waned, so has the spectacle become a little boring.

As this dawned on me, I knew that with a series of jet suits customized in such a way that they were race-ready, there was a possibility Gravity Industries might have the power to create a Formula One-style event all of its own with heaps of drama. In the same way that Formula One has a circus-like theatre it transports around the world comprising constructors, innovators, engineers and drivers, celebrating the ingenuity and humanity of each one, why couldn't we do something similar, but with jet suits? The commercial opportunities of such a move seemed huge, the perfect way of building the Gravity brand and funding our R&D plans for the future.

I had answered the question. I had found *the point.*

As the idea for a Gravity Race Series took root, my mind played with all the possibilities. Instead of just flying the jet suit alone in the air for the entertainment of thousands, I wanted to create a racing format and a series of teams that could involve and entertain vast crowds, both live and hopefully through televised races. To begin with, every racer would use an existing Gravity jet suit, but as the competition evolved other engineers might decide to build rival systems to compete against us. Each competing team would have an accessible element behind its distinct brand in their pilots and their personalities; fans could celebrate the individuals they connected with most keenly, just as F1 fans follow Lewis Hamilton or Sebastian Vettel. Meanwhile, each team would also appeal to fans on a technological level, as they attempted to build a faster suit than their rivals. Like all great sporting events, my idea carried an almost gladiatorial spirit – there was danger and a certain thrilling appeal.

I'd learned from doing so many events around the world that the suit delivers a wow factor. My displays became an excellent way of polling perceptions, and the demographic was wide-ranging, featuring everybody from three-year-olds to leading business figures. Every time somebody watched a flight for the first time, they tended to have the same experience: *Jesus Christ, I didn't think it was going to be that intense.* The visceral power generated by the engines helped. As with all my engineering obsessions when growing up as a kid, the suit had the noise and it carried the drama; many people also made the useful link to Iron Man, a superhero icon. Meanwhile the human experience was very much front and centre. People watching from

Bournemouth Beach or at a launch in China were able to see my face quite easily as I flew. I wasn't moving around in a faceless piece of machinery, a capsule of metal and glass 5,000 feet up in the air.

I needed to build the right conditions for what might become a brand-new sport. I was determined that the format should be both compelling and dramatic so that every event could be filmed, broadcast and shared, but every step towards realizing my idea raised more questions. I needed to design the sport in such a way that our races didn't look half baked, or shoddy. But how should we do it?

The first issue was pilots. I already had two ready to go, one of whom was Angelo, the other myself. We also began training a number of other potential candidates throughout 2019. It became clear that the best pilots were lightweight, fit, spatially aware and typically had some background in flying, extreme sports or gymnastics. This was the inspiration behind approaching the well-respected Basingstoke Gymnastics Club. Gymnasts Ryan, Jamie and Paul proved to be excellent pilots, with Ryan notably flying without the tether on his third three-minute training run! Our constant enhancements to the suit have also made it easier to control, and consequently easier to fly. We also invested in an all-weather training barn in which people could familiarize themselves with the technology quickly and effectively. Thanks to this facility, Alex Wilson and Sam Rogers, the two lead engineers in the team, soon became highly proficient pilots. But these developments required more jet suits. *How could I build them efficiently and at speed?* Well, I solved that problem by designing the suit in such a way that some of the components, such as hand-held sleeves that contain the turbines, could be 3D-printed externally, which sped up the production process significantly. We've since designed the entire backpack structure for 3D printing too, and continue to make further enhancements.

Other issues were solved along the way. I bought a horsetruck, a luxurious version of the kind you see riding up and down the motorway with a trio of race stallions bumping up and down inside. The vehicle was designed to carry both riders and beasts in comfort. There was even a lounge area inside. We then converted it into a mobile unit for Gravity Industries in which I could transport jet suits and equipment around the country. I would have been entirely justified in spending over £120,000 on an all-bells-and-whistles, customized, Team Oakley-style vehicle with dry ice and lasers. Instead I spent thirty grand, maintaining the bootstrap spirit that has served us well so far, knowing that if everything went wrong I could sell the vehicle the following day, recouping most of the costs. That has very much been my preferred way of working throughout. For every foray into making suits, selling suits, flight training and live events, we have rapidly dived into most ideas, but have always started small, working in financial figures that I knew would be recoverable if an idea proves unworkable.

The next question, however, was this: how to create a race format that was as exciting as Formula One, or Red Bull's X-Games events? I knew that the race had to be held over water for dramatic and safety purposes. Such an environment would create a spectacle because pilots were bound to crash spectacularly into the drink, while at the same time the water massively reduced the risk of a serious injury befalling anyone tumbling from the sky, while retaining an element of danger for the watching audience. We also planned to enhance each race with a series of obstacles placed into the path of the competitors. This would significantly raise the dramatic value of each race. The potential for thrills and spills was high.

I then used my platform to subtly plug the concept, mentioning it in talks and presentations. Name-dropping the idea of a race series sparked the imagination of investors and media production companies, who soon reached out to us. Cities offered to host races, regardless of whether we'd secured broadcasting rights or not. At least twelve broadcasters did register their interest in the early stages, a number of them big hitters with the potential to reach a huge proportion of the world's population. Given attention of that kind it's very easy to feel flattered, but I knew I wanted to launch the race series on my own terms, as I'd done with the suit. Rather than show them a series of DIY video clips we had cobbled together – a demonstration of how

233

the product might look to a watching audience – I decided to opt for high-end production values. With drones, we produced a short film of 360-degree footage as I and another pilot negotiated a course of custom-built obstacles, such as inflatable turning posts and gates, positioned on the Lagoona Park lake in Reading.

There was also the idea that other companies could join the race series as rival constructors, in the same way that Formula One has Ferrari, McLaren, Red Bull and Mercedes. We have a list of companies asking to participate that far exceeds the slots initially available. We also have an intimate working relationship with our engine developer. They were very cooperative when modifying the designs of our micro turbines, but they could quite easily create a different engine as a rival to the Gravity Industries team and become a part of the race series. As in Formula One, different vehicles have different characteristics. I envisioned a time when a similar set-up might occur in jet suit technology. And as long as the event remains competitive, it makes for a very exciting development and will raise awareness of Gravity Industries' innovations and output.

Throughout this planning stage everything was under our control, which was exactly how I liked it. I didn't want to haggle with TV companies, looking for deals and negotiating investment. Instead I used the money earned from my public appearances and displays, and the revenue received from the sale of jet suits and flight experiences, to fund our race R&D. This was quite an audacious approach, but it soon began to pay dividends. We progressed the concept. Slowly, investors caught up to the idea and asked to be involved. A typical pathway for a project of this nature would be to spend nine months on the road to raise £20 million and then go dark for a year, working feverishly on the concept, hoping it matched the expectations promised to investors. I didn't want to be in a position where I couldn't deliver on a partner's expectations, because that would have left me having to spend another six months running around, begging my investors to accept a modified plan.

But under the development concept we have I didn't need to answer to anybody. Gravity Industries was able to adapt and evolve at its own pace. I wanted to find new pilots at the right time. I wanted to develop our courses and race obstacles on our terms, and have the freedom to experiment and innovate without any external pressure. I was eager to see if we could bring off a spectacular racing event, with everything completed under our own terms and conditions. My race series was going ahead, whether it was purely for the entertainment of a few hundred people or a global audience of millions.

Workshop Notes

CREATE YOUR HALO EFFECT

As we developed Gravity Industries, I became very conscious that shoving our ideas or theories into people's faces was a bad thing. Instead I wanted to give them something material, an existing and exciting concept for the public, and the commercial world, to pick up and run with if they wanted to – like the idea of the race series. I've presented at too many tech conferences where the guy before me has talked about crypto-currency AI or blockchain, passionately describing how the dollar has died or robots are taking over. Following my talk, a person then details the possibilities of asteroid mining. All of it very inspiring and thought-provoking, but largely unproven. Instead, I talk about what we've actually done. I want to prove, not predict. Having something real to demonstrate an idea is much more powerful.

    There was something very impactful about introducing a person to an exciting concept that had already secured a momentum of its own – that the high-speed train was leaving the station and anyone wanting to catch it had to move fast.

Think of this in the context of the TV show *Dragons' Den*. The unappealing contestant says, 'I've got this amazing concept, which I think will be a super success. Can I have some money to see if it works?' That's not a very compelling argument. But the successful person sets an interesting narrative. They say, 'We've worked our guts out and managed to sell half a million units to a retailer . . . We need help scaling up to meet demand.' Suddenly the dragons are tripping over themselves. To their thinking, the opportunity is clear. I wanted that same ethos to come through in everything we did, particularly the race series, which we've created with a similar attitude. *We're doing this anyway and you should come along for the ride.*

I wanted Gravity Industries to make the most of the Halo Effect, as a result of which a person (or in this case a business) takes on a more attractive hue because of their personality or image, and their early successes. This is something we've cultivated at Gravity Industries by being very different. People believe that because we've innovated a unique product we must be going somewhere, so they jump on board. Collaborating with interesting people and companies has been a lot of fun, and also helped us break new ground.

One of the reasons we've managed to do this is that I've never gone into a meeting with the objective of securing money. Instead, I've shown an investor or influential person the workings of what is an outrageously fun project to be a part of, something that we're going to continue to grow regardless of their help. That is a very powerful action, because most investors and decision makers are used to being bombarded with business plans, financial projections and slide decks. People want their money, and the implicit desperation is such a turn-off.

What has become clear through the creative process and the adventures I've experienced is that I'm now even more in tune with my late father's ambitions and dreams. He was an aeronautical engineer, an innovator and a designer; his passion was for unusual and creative ideas that could be commercialized. As I grew up, Dad's interest in aeronautics and flight was hugely influential. In my lab there's a picture hanging on the wall. It's a drawing of my father on a bicycle, a hang-glider wing attached to his back. It was given to him as an office leaving present. Sometimes I look at that photograph and marvel at the similarity of our lives. *It's as if he knew.*

I often wonder at our differing trajectories, though. Latterly I've attempted some self-analysis: *to what extent has my path matched his?* I know I've never wanted to experience the hardships he suffered. I wouldn't want to put my family through the same pain and I'd hate for my kids to feel the insecurity I experienced while growing up. And yet, I've very much placed myself in the same line of fire. I guess you could compare it to somebody's dad passing away on a trip to the North Pole, only for that person to then spend their entire life trying to traverse the Arctic themselves.

To extend the analogy, *I've made it to my North Pole.* I've achieved some of the things Dad didn't, and that experience has been both unnerving and hugely rewarding, to such an extent that I now find myself in quite unusual surroundings. I've made it to what I believed was the final destination, stuck my flag in the ice. But what comes next? I currently find myself in uncharted territory, but the possibilities in terms of where the suit and Gravity Industries will go next are endless. So let's explore what our jet suits might achieve over the next few years.

The development of a new sport is very much in place, and how the public reacts to the race series will undoubtedly shape our future, but the other areas in which I might move are equally thrilling. In January 2019 I flew across the infamous Royal Marine Commandos assault course in Lympstone, buzzing over what was a gruelling set of obstacles in a matter of seconds, proving to the Navy what was possible with jet suit technology. Within twenty-four hours, the resulting video had been shared among the world's military on social media, including by the former Special Forces operative-turned-TV survival expert Bear Grylls. I've often noticed how any connection with the military has created a mystique for what I'm doing. It's as if I'm operating from the shadows in some way.

I'd imagine a lot of that comes from the James Bond movies, where quirky Secret Service characters such as Q have long presented 007 with various gadgets designed to help him escape from hair-raising scrapes. In the 1965 film *Thunderball*, Bond – played by Sean Connery – even makes a getaway using a jetpack, and the technology was real back then, although based on a terrifying peroxide rocket engine – hard to control and with an aggressive burn time of ninety seconds. As we've advanced the design from our workshop, I've realized the jet suit has some potential as a military asset, particularly for anyone involved in marine assaults, such as the Special Boat Service.

At present, Commandos and the SBS storm enemy vessels either by approaching in a small boat before attaching assault ladders to a target or by helicoptering in and descending from fast ropes. For such operations, a jet suit presents an interesting option. It's quick. It's precise. Most of all it delivers shock and awe, and delivers any number of independently mobile operatives without the single-point failure risk of a boat or helicopter. We have even been asked about the feasibility of a shoulder-mounted weapon and to assess whether military forces using the suit could carry one; delivering suppressing fire while coming in to land is one way for jet suit pilots to protect themselves from hostile forces. Elsewhere, this same technology could be used by rescue operators such as the coastguard or emergency services; without the weaponry it would be possible for a jet suit pilot to fly on to a ship in distress, extracting passengers or delivering assistance in tricky conditions.

In the meantime, we have made inroads into the possibility of developing an electric suit because it's such an appealing area: it would be quieter and far quicker to start up, without any exhaust fumes. The biggest challenge with an electric model is the energy density. To fly on jet fuel we have to fill two tanks; at present, to fly on an electric source, we need a significantly greater weight in lithium batteries. But we haven't allowed the restrictions to dishearten us. Instead we've kept ahead of the curve by starting our R&D in this area with the view that with electric motor and battery technology advancing at such a rapid rate, we'll be in place to make the next leap quite quickly.

It's within this area that I'd like to investigate the possibility of developing a tethered version of the jet suit for a theme park environment. I'm also fascinated by what we might achieve with smaller components and variants of the suit in the parkour and extreme sport communities.

But the next obvious step in a world of doing not very obvious things is the introduction of wings to the current suit, which we have been exploring since 2018. These additions might act as air brakes, though they're more likely to alter the way we fly: if my theories are right, adding wings will give the pilot a natural uplift. I discovered as much when I first flapped that buzzard's wing at home. I've since attempted flight with hang-glider wings attached to my back, and I've worn wingsuit webbing between my legs. Both have lifted me into the air with varying degrees of success. If we're able to get the design right, this innovation might help to save on fuel consumption – the less fuel a pilot expends while staying in the air, the more fuel they'll have available to move around once they're up there, allowing them to fly for longer, over further distances.

Ultimately, the big dream for many of our fans is personal transport – a world in which people are able to fly to the shops, or around their garden, in a jet suit. It's a nice idea, and the technology could support it, but it would be hard to eliminate the serious risk of operator error and abuse.

That said, people laughed when it was suggested that the first motorcars might be used for mass transport. Bertha Benz proved them all wrong. Who's to say we can't do something similar with a jet suit and some left-field thinking?

A strange thing happens when a person becomes successful, or gains recognition for doing something they love: Imposter's Syndrome kicks in. It's the very real dread that convinces you that at any time an officious figure might knock on your door. Glumly, he or she will announce, 'Mr Browning, we've realized you're just a former trader wandering around trying to invent a new way of flying. Can you please stop all work and allow the anointed innovators of the world to make the innovations? Get back to reality.' This is an emotion experienced by many people who do jobs they are passionate about. I suspect it stems from a fear of loss and the idea of being forced into a line of work less exciting or worthwhile. I've sometimes experienced this concern myself, usually after a successful event or a breakthrough in the lab. However, I've often tempered that sense of self-doubt with what I call the Innovator's Delusion, the other 50 per cent of our brain that says, *Of course I can bloody well do this.*

That was the joyous and terrifying equation applicable to everything I did at the beginning of this journey, and everything I do now. The joy came from the realization that Red Bull and *Wired* wanted to feature my work on their platforms, or that I was to appear in the *Guinness Book of World Records*, a volume opened by a large number of school-age kids on Christmas Day. The reverse emotion was the worry that my ride might be derailed by bad luck, or an accident that made me the laughing stock of social media. To overcome that fear I constantly reminded myself of the successes; I used my triumphs as two fingers to stick up at the voices and doubts that occasionally whispered, *This is never going to work*. And sure, there's no way of knowing whether a product will deliver success. But telling myself I am on the right path, while observing what's going on in my business, is the only option.

It's worked out pretty well so far.

Through a period of trial and error, both Gravity Industries and myself have gone from strength to strength since our inception in 2017. The lessons I've learned along the way, and imparted here, have served to enhance what was initially an ambitious and unusual idea: would it be possible to reimagine the way human beings thought about flying? The answer has been yes, but that has only increased the scale of my ambition. Meanwhile, so many more challenges and questions have emerged since that first flight across a farmyard in Salisbury. Locating the answers will define where I go next, but if life has taught me anything, it's that time and innovation will inevitably reveal a roadmap of interesting new ideas and solutions.

Whatever route I take, I intend to fly there.

Covid update

This book was due to be published in 2020, but due to the pandemic and the impact on the publishing industry, it was postponed. However, it does give me the opportunity to briefly update you on progress over this most troublesome of years for us all.

Having delivered over a hundred commercial events across more than thirty countries, the Gravity Team and I were three weeks away from flying to Bermuda to launch the inaugural event of the Jet Suit Race Series. But in March 2020, the world shut down. Subsequently, we saw every one of our lucrative summer-season events fall by the wayside. I'm proud that in response we refocused and employed our 3d printer to run off more than 150 face visors for the local healthcare community before supplies stabilized, but we felt helpless initially.

As a team, we aren't very good at sitting still, and it dawned on me pretty quickly that our restless approach to innovation and our adaptability were key in this environment. There aren't, of course, many guidebooks on how to run a successful and profitable jet-suit business, so these traits had become part of our ethos and were about to pay dividends.

Over Zoom we actually accelerated the R&D programme, taking advantage of the now empty diary to make huge leaps with things like the tethered electric training suit and the spectacular third generation jet suit. We had time to focus properly on the requirements for Search & Rescue and the tactical military community. Relationships with big brands started to flourish as we had more time to scale up our social media footprint across multiple platforms. The @GravityIndustries YouTube channel has had tens of millions of views, and the @TakeOnGravity handle on Facebook, Instagram, TikTok and even Linkedin represents many huge communities.

At the time of writing its mid-January 2021, and I've just celebrated my forty-second birthday. The UK is in the midst of the worst Covid rates so far, but vaccines are being administered at an ever-faster rate. We all hope this is the beginning of the end of this global nightmare.

The future feels uncertain, but Gravity is in a great place. This is testament to a remarkable team and the relentless and passionate support from the public and media. We have a bright and exciting future and it will take more than Covid to stop us in our ambition to reimagine human flight and seek to inspire the next generation to dare ask, 'What if?'

Takeaways

○ It's easy to feel like an imposter, especially when we're successful or having fun on a project we're developing. Instead we must remind ourselves of the hard work and successes we've experienced so far. It diminishes the fear that we're not worthy of our position.

○ Create a Halo Effect. Become appealing by giving the impression your projects are worthy of investment by treating them with confidence. We're excited about the work, so it must be worthwhile. We're pressing ahead with an exciting adventure regardless, so it must be an avenue worth pursuing.

○ Be ready to show your progress. Too many people discuss the future of their business plans or ideas without presenting a context for the now. Crypto-currency innovators talk about the latest digital monetary unit and how it signals the death of the dollar, but they rarely present a graspable benefit for the present day. It's far better to have a sense of current progress so investors and adopters can feel what it is we're doing, rather than merely having to imagine its potential.

○ Change is inevitable, yet most of us instinctively mourn the loss of the familiar and even linger in denial, disbelief and depression. Notice that instinct can move on as quickly as we can, towards acceptance and adaptation. Change always creates new opportunities, even as it squashes the status quo. Successful innovators and entrepreneurs aren't afraid to keep trying – and often failing – in their attempts to seek out these new opportunities. No matter what life throws at us.

243

ACKNOWLEDGEMENTS

Although I started out alone on the path towards exploring a new chapter in human flight, it would not have been possible to achieve without the vast number of passionate, enthusiastic, incredible people who surround me and this journey.

Initially I was supported by my wife Debbie and father-in-law Sam. Both helped me get through the first few months of creating and testing the endless prototypes.

As a new business we were very grateful to our first investors who took a punt on us, Anthony Ganjou and Tim and Adam Draper, who had the vision at an early stage and fuelled our swift progress. While still iterating the prototype we were helped along by the talented John Reese and Mike Lloyd who bridged my knowledge gap around the electronics control system.

Next to come on board was aeronautics graduate Alex Wilson, who took on more of the electronics, design and general suit engineering. Alex was soon joined by Sam Rogers, a talented CAD designer and Additive manufacturing engineer. Together these two are a formidable pair, both brilliant engineers as well as accomplished jet suit pilots, veterans of many international events between them.

Huge thanks go to my dedicated, diligent commercial and events team, Maria Vildavskaya and Katy Crudgington, who at the time of writing have delivered almost a hundred events across a barely believable thirty countries in less than three years. Meanwhile, the endlessly talented Anthony Quinn has led our STEM agenda, ensuring our passion reaches and inspires school-aged kids. We are equally thankful to Lee Crudgington, Red Devils display lead and social media point man, and to Laura for leading on Gravity clothing and merchandise.

Across the pond we are extremely grateful to our enthusiastic US team, with Chris Goslin at the helm. The US has been the focus of a huge amount of Gravity's activity, California being a second home for the company.

Thanks, too, to our brilliant duo of pilots, Jamie Stanley and Ryan Hopgood, for taking time out from stunt work and GB gymnastics to fly for us. And to Paul Jones and our cohort of hard-working supporters – from PhD students to military test pilots to stunt men – who regularly assist us at events: Abhishek, Lewis, Kyle, Dan, Dave and Tucker. All contribute their time, boundless energy and knowledge to our project.

I should also mention the invaluable assistance of those who have supported our flight training and development: Old Sarum Airfield, Hurst Castle, Fonthill Estate, Lord Pembroke and Wilton House, Nick Hankey, the Goodwood team and, most importantly, Hugh, Lucinda and Stephen, who provided us with our local farm test site. Without these locations this journey really wouldn't have left the drawing board.

Lastly, I wish to acknowledge the amazing Angelo Grubisic, Gravity's second ever pilot. He stepped up and proved that others could quickly learn to fly the jet suit, and he did so with an infectiously positive attitude, always full of joy and excitement. Such a spirit will be sorely missed. To quote him, 'If you are not doing what you love, you are the foolish one.'

PICTURE
ACKNOWLEDGEMENTS

All photographs are provided courtesy of the author unless otherwise stated. Every effort has been made to trace copyright holders and clear permission for additional images. The author and the publisher would welcome the opportunity to correct any omissions in this respect.

Second section

Page 2: Richard speaking on stage: © TED.

Pages 4–5: All photographs at Farnborough International Airshow: © Rich Cooper; Bournemouth Air Festival: © Waveslider Photography; Royal Navy International Air Day: © Edwin Van Keulen.

Page 6: Flying off Hurst Castle: © Chris Russell Photography; Setting a new speed record in 2019: © Guinness World Records.

Page 7: At the HMS *Sultan* STEM day: © Crown.

ABOUT THE AUTHOR

Richard Browning is the founder of human propulsion technology start-up Gravity Industries Ltd, which he founded in March 2017 after inventing, building and patenting an 'Iron Man-like' flight system, the Gravity Jet Suit.

A former Royal Marines Reservist, Richard worked on a number of game-changing innovations during his sixteen year oil trading career with BP in the City of London, before rediscovering a family passion for invention, engineering and aviation.

His inspiration and vision for Gravity is in large part a tribute to his father, Michael Browning, an aeronautical engineer and maverick inventor, who tragically died when Richard was a teenager.